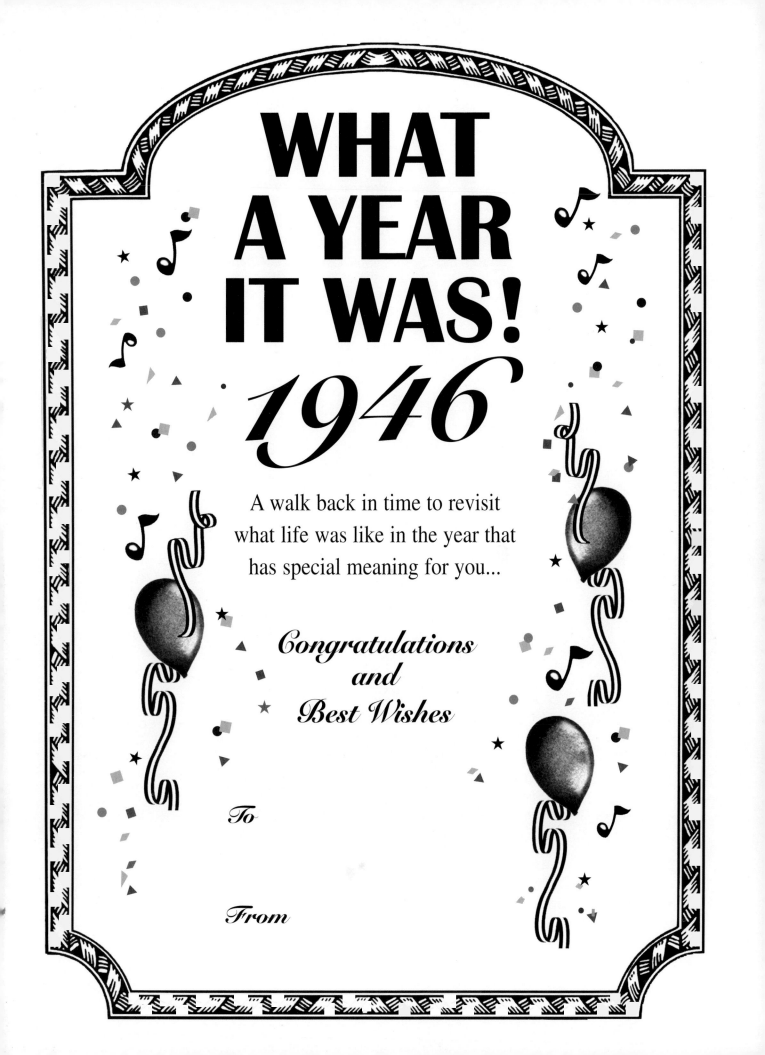

WHAT A YEAR IT WAS!

1946

A walk back in time to revisit
what life was like in the year that
has special meaning for you...

*Congratulations
and
Best Wishes*

To

From

DEDICATION

To My Children—Lee, Laurie, Melanie And Sweet Danielle
Thank You For Your Love, Support And Sense Of Humor

Designer • Peter Hess
Production Supervisor • Carol Davis
Researcher • Laurie Cohn

CONTENTS

POLITICS AND WORLD EVENTS

1946

UNITED NATIONS SECURITY COUNCIL HOLDS FIRST SESSION IN LONDON

Edward R. Stettinius *(above right)*, United States delegate, shaking hands with British representative, Ernest Bevin attends this historic session.

Also in attendance for this important 11-member council is Russia's delegate, Andrei Gromyko.

WHAT A YEAR IT WAS!

5

POLAND REBUILDS HER SHATTERED CITY

Warsaw, one of the first major European cities to fall under the Nazi blitz, embarks on rebuilding its capital.

After six years of war, some semblance of normal life begins to return to this war-torn city.

U.S. SUPREME COURT JUSTICES CALL FOR TOLERANCE

Supporting the American Brotherhood campaign, sponsored by the National Council of Christians and Jews, Justice Frankfurter states that:

"The unfolding of our Republic is the story of the greatest racial mixture in history. Of the 56 signers of the Declaration of Independence, 18 were of non-English stock... Foreign-born citizens of almost every land fought in the war for independence, helped save the union and in conspicuous numbers are found on the honor rolls of the two World Wars."

Chief Justice Harlan Stone in his plea for tolerance added:

"Freedom of the mind and the spirit has its practical aspects in everyday life. It includes the right of every man to live and work in peace, to earn and to save and to enjoy the fruits of his labor, so long as their enjoyment does no harm to his neighbor..."

AMERICA has THE WORLD'S BIGGEST BOMBER!

B-36
Photographed on
recent test flight

THIS is the giant B-36—the biggest land-based bomber ever built.

Manned by a crew of 15 men, it is designed to carry 10,000 pounds of bombs 10,000 miles. Its top speed is more than 300 miles per hour. Operating from airports available to us, the B-36 could, *if this country were attacked,* drop bombs on any city in the world.

Just how big is "the world's biggest bomber"?

Imagine a tail fin that is almost as tall as the average 5-story apartment building! Fuel tanks so large that more than 2 railroad tank cars are needed to fill them! Six pusher-type engines with a total of 18,000 horsepower! A wingspread as great as that of two B-24 Liberator bombers, with 10 feet to spare!

Designed and built by Consolidated Vultee, in conjunction with the United States Army Air Forces, the mammoth B-36 is a mighty symbol of peace-loving America's determination to remain strong in the air—to preserve the peace through strength!

The awe-inspiring B-36—first of a fleet of such long-range bombers now under construction—is one of Consolidated Vultee's important contributions to this nation's protective strength in the air.

And THE WORLD'S MOST MODERN TWIN-ENGINE AIRLINER is on the way!

CONVAIR 240

America's leadership in commercial aviation is a *must,* too.

Consolidated Vultee is now building the most modern twin-engine airliner the world has ever seen. This new transport, known as the Convair-240, will be flying the skyways next summer.

Many famous airlines—including American Airlines, Western Air Lines, Pan American World Airways, Continental Air Lines, and KLM (Royal Dutch Airlines) have already ordered fleets of Convair-240's.

Watch for this ultra-modern 300 MPH airliner—pressurized and air conditioned for your comfort.

We promise you that your first flight in the Convair-240 will be an experience you will want to repeat over and over again—whenever you want to travel *faster,* and with *greater safety* and *comfort!*

Let's keep America strong in the air!

Consolidated Vultee Aircraft Corporation

San Diego, California · Downey, California · Wayne, Michigan (Stinson Division) · Fort Worth, Texas · Nashville, Tennessee

At the request of President Truman, former president Herbert Hoover prepares to leave New York for Europe where his task is finding ways of averting starvation in nations torn by war.

Hoover In Italy

Mr. Hoover arrives in Rome and is greeted by Italian food minister de Gaspari.

WHAT A YEAR IT WAS!

In Italy, the work of the United Nations Relief Agency is already in effect as thousands of school children are fed daily under the supervision of the school authorities.

Flanked by John W. Snyder *(left)*, Director, and O.M. Garner, Chairman of the War Mobilization and Reconversion Advisory Board, President Truman approves resolution by board members endorsing a loan to Britain.

PRESIDENT TRUMAN FAVORS LOAN TO GREAT BRITAIN

President Truman calls the agreement:

"Good business for the industries of America, good business for our farmers, and good business for our workers...an important step in rebuilding foreign trade and in creating jobs in America. The alternative to the British loan is trade warfare between nations. Peace can be built only on a foundation of world economic cooperation and stability. The British loan is a cornerstone in the world's structure of peace."

13

1946

NAZI WAR CRIMINALS SENTENCED AT NUREMBERG TRIALS

Death Sentence:	Bormann, Frank, Frick, Goering*, Jodl, Kaltenbrunner, Keitel, Ribbentrop, Rosenberg, Sauckel, Seyss-Inquart, Streicher
Life Imprisonment:	Funk, Hess, Raeder
20 Years Imprisonment:	Schirach, Speer
15 Years Imprisonment:	Neurath
10 Years Imprisonment:	Doenitz
Acquittals:	Fritsche, Schacht, von Papen

Goering Commits Suicide The Night Before His Execution.

Attempts To Revive The Nazi Party Crushed By Allies Who Seize 1,000 Sympathizers.

Argentina Provides Safe Haven For Nazis.

WHAT A YEAR IT WAS!

Pan American Generals Tour U.S. Bases

At the invitation of our Secretary of War, generals from Pan American countries are touring United States camps and bases.

Airborne troops demonstrate their training exercises at Fort Benning, Georgia.

Mexico's defense minister shows particular interest in a flame-thrower. The generals agree that a modern army equipped with modern weapons will enable them to join in keeping the peace.

1946

PRESIDENT TRUMAN CALLS FOR AMERICANS TO REDUCE FOOD CONSUMPTION TO HELP IN WORLD HUNGER FIGHT

EXCERPTS FROM SPEECH GIVEN APRIL 19, 1946.

"It is my duty to join my voice with the voices of humanity everywhere in behalf of the starving millions of human beings all over the world. We have a high responsibility, as Americans, to go to their rescue...

"We would not be Americans if we did not wish to share our comparative plenty with suffering people...

"America cannot remain healthy and happy in the same world where millions of human beings are starving...

"...we would all be better off physically and spiritually, if we ate less... Every slice of bread, every ounce of fat and oil saved by your voluntary sacrifice, will help keep starving people alive.

"By our combined effort, we will reduce starvation and with God's help, we will avert the worst of this plague of famine that follows in the wake of war. I ask every American now to pledge himself to share..."

➠ **President Truman Creates Central Intelligence Group.**

➠ **Chester Bowles Heads Newly Created Office Of Economic Stabilization.**

➠ **W. Averell Harriman Named U.S. Ambassador To Britain.**

➠ **U.S. Supreme Court Rules Segregation In Public Transportation Unconstitutional.**

➠ **President Truman Warns Future Atomic Wars "...*May Well Destroy Nations And Change Present Standard Of Civilization.*"**

➠ **President Truman Creates The Atomic Energy Commission.**

➠ **Wisconsin Elects Joe McCarthy To The Senate.**

➠ **President Truman Appoints Ambassador W. Averell Harriman Secretary Of Commerce Replacing Henry A. Wallace.**

➠ **Republicans Regain Control Of Congress.**

➠ **Supreme Court Grants Oregon Indians Land Payment Rights From The U.S. Government.**

➠ **December: President Truman Formally Ends World War II.**

- Italy Grants Women Voting Rights.

- Italians Vote For Republic Form Of Government In First Free Election Since 1922—King Umberto II Leaves Italy.

- Emperor Hirohito Disclaims His Own Divinity.

- Japan's Former Premier, General Hideki Tojo And 27 Other Defendants Go On Trial In Tokyo For War Crimes.

Emperor Hirohito Spared War Crimes Trial By Allies.

Women Exercise Right To Vote In Japan For The First Time.

U.S. Announces It Will Stay In Korea Until The Country Is Free And Unified.

President Truman Pledges Aid For The Philippines As The Nation Becomes An Independent Republic.

Soviet Union And Switzerland Resume Diplomatic Relations After 22-Year Break.

Britain And France Withdraw From Syria.

Ho Chi Minh Wins North Vietnamese Elections.

French Government Declares Martial Law In Vietnam As Full-Scale War Becomes Imminent.

21-Nation Peace Conference Opens In Paris To Discuss Peace Treaties For Italy, Hungary, Rumania, Bulgaria and Finland.

Divers and other salvage workers operate around the clock, taking advantage of low tides when water can be pumped out of the hulks.

Post-War Salvage Operations Proceed Quickly To Clear Vital Shipping Lanes Of Sunken Ships In British Harbors

These pumps are capable of handling thousands of gallons of water a minute and have helped in the raising of hundreds of vessels.

When the ship has been floated, it is towed to the nearest beach where further salvage operations are conducted.

Everything usable is saved for the rebuilding of Britain's shattered Merchant Marine.

On the other side of the North Sea is another ship graveyard filled with German wrecks.

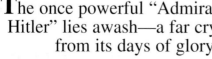

The once powerful "Admiral Hitler" lies awash—a far cry from its days of glory.

1946

Britain Imposes Curfew On Jewish Community In Tel Aviv Following Death Of Seven British Soldiers In Palestine.

Jewish State Rejected By The Anglo-American Committee Of Inquiry On Jewish Problems In Europe And Palestine.

Irgun, Under Leadership of Menachem Begin, Claims Responsibility For Attack On British Headquarters At King David Hotel In Jerusalem, Citing Suppression Of Immigration Of Jews.

British Troops Isolate Tel Aviv In Search Of Zionist Guerrillas.

Jewish Protestors Sing The Jewish National Anthem, "Hatikva," In Protest Over British "Operation Igloo," The Deportation To Cyprus Of Jewish Immigrants Seeking Refuge In Palestine From European Persecution.

Truman Urges Britain To Open Palestine To Jewish Refugees Who Immigrated Illegally Seeking Sanctuary From European Oppression And Throws His Support Behind A Jewish State. Arabs Accuse Him Of Betrayal.

London Conference On Palestine Boycotted By Jews And Arabs.

THIS NEW INTERNATIONAL
GETS THERE FASTER WITH MORE

Here's new cruising speed for American truck transport—new highway speed and new maintained speed over the hills—maintained speed that earns greater profit per ton mile.

It's the new International KR-12, a heavy-duty highway truck-tractor driven by a larger, more powerful, war-proved engine—586 cubic-inch piston displacement.

It delivers new standards of maintained speed in hilly country because its high ratio of horsepower to gross weight makes possible almost constant use of high speed gears. Nor does engine torque drop off suddenly to cut road speed. Instead, 450 pounds-feet of torque are maintained from 900 to 1600 engine revolutions per minute.

It is equipped with special heavy-duty axles and transmissions to handle its added power.

It operates with almost passenger car ease, despite its 28,500 pound gross vehicle weight rating.

This speed-merchant of the hills and highways is the latest addition to the *complete* International line—everything for highway and off-highway work from half-ton pickups to off-highway haulers with gross vehicle weight ratings up to 45 tons.

The new KR-12 represents more than 40 years' truck manufacturing experience. It shares this outstanding International record—more heavy-duty International Trucks purchased for commerce and industry in the last 15 years than any other make.

It is backed by the truck industry's outstanding

service facilities—service supplied by International Truck Dealers everywhere and by a network of International Branches that form the nation's largest company-owned truck-service organization.

It's an International Truck, this KR-12, packed with all the name, International, means, and with maintained hill and highway speed that cuts travel time and steps up operating profits.

Motor Truck Division
INTERNATIONAL HARVESTER COMPANY
180 North Michigan Avenue   Chicago 1, Illinois

INTERNATIONAL TRUCKS

Tune in "Harvest of Stars" every Sunday, NBC Network.
See newspapers for time and station.

Stalin Announces Five-Year Plan For U.S.S.R.

Pravda Denounces Churchill As Anti-Soviet Warmonger.

Winston Churchill Makes "Iron Curtain" Speech.

Soviet Spy Ring Uncovered In Canada.

Russia Agrees To Withdraw Troops From Iran. Accord Granting The U.S.S.R. 51% Control Of Oil For 25 Years Revealed By Tehran.

American Killed By Soviet Police For Photographing An Election In Berlin.

Bread Rationing Begins In Great Britain.

U.S. Charges The Soviet Union Of Stripping Hungary Of Needed Resources.

2.5 Million Pounds Of Clothing For European Relief Donated By New Yorkers.

President Truman Creates 9-Step Program To Feed Europeans.

Argentina's Col. Juan D. Peron Wins Sufficient Electoral Votes To Land Him Presidency. He Is Installed As 29th President Of Argentina.

Argentina And Soviet Union Resume Diplomatic Relations After 28-Year Break.

60-Day Siege Of War Declared In Chile.

Mao Tse-tung Orders Showdown With Chiang Kai-shek.

U. S. And China Sign Treaty Of Peace.

Mob Violence Escalates In Cairo As Egyptians Riot To Protest British Rule.

The British Flag Is Lowered For The Last Time In Cairo After 64 Years.

THE UNITED NATIONS

- The League Of Nations Is Officially Dissolved In A Vote By 34 Nations In Geneva.

- First Session Of United Nations General Assembly Held In London.

- Site Of The World's Fair In Flushing Meadows, New York Designated As Temporary Home For The U.N. General Assembly.

- New York Declared Permanent Home Of The United Nations.

- John D. Rockefeller, Jr. Donates $8.5 Million Site For Permanent Headquarters.

- Statesman Bernard Baruch Appointed U.S. Representative To U.N. Atomic Energy Commission.

- Bernard Baruch Asks For U.N. Control Of A-Bomb.

- U.N. Security Council Condemns Franco Of Spain.

1946

- CHARLES DEGAULLE RESIGNS AS PRESIDENT OF FRANCE.
- GREEK KING GEORGE II RESTORED TO THRONE IN LANDSLIDE AFTER REFERENDUM TO RETAIN MONARCHY.
- HUNGARY PROCLAIMED A REPUBLIC.
- 60 INDIANS KILLED AND MORE THAN 500 INJURED IN BLOODY ANTI-BRITISH PROTESTS IN BOMBAY. 300,000 JOIN IN DEMONSTRATION.
- ATTLEE OFFERS INDIA FULL INDEPENDENCE AFTER AGREEMENT ON CONSTITUTION.
- NEHRU APPOINTED HEAD OF INDIA'S INTERIM GOVERNMENT.

NOBEL PEACE PRIZE

Emily G. Balch
&
John R. Mott

PASSINGS

MIKHAIL IVANOVICH KALININ, President Of The Soviet Union For 27 Years, Dies At 70.

HARRY HOPKINS, Top Aide And Confidante To President Franklin D. Roosevelt, Dies In New York At 55.

HARLAN F. STONE, Chief Justice Of The United States, Dies At 73.

WHAT A YEAR IT WAS!

P
E
O
P
L
E

Margaret Rose, youngest daughter of Britain's King and Queen, makes her first public appearance by herself.

The Princess Goes Public

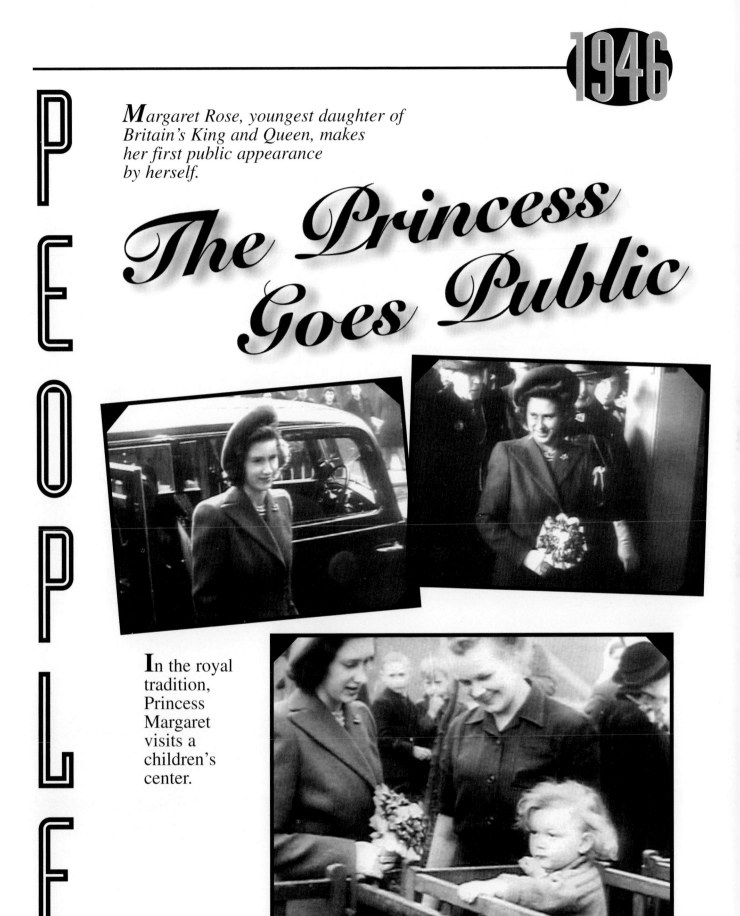

In the royal tradition, Princess Margaret visits a children's center.

Riding a trusty white steed, Admiral Halsey arrives for the initiation ceremony into Saints and Sinners.

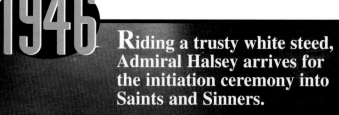

ADMIRAL HALSEY INITIATED INTO SAINTS AND SINNERS

General Doolittle and former President Battista of Cuba observe the festivities.

Admiral Halsey thanks the audience as he is formally welcomed into their group.

A rousing send-up of Hitler and Hirohito adds to the evening's festivities.

WHAT A YEAR IT WAS!

Background for Beauty!

The New Ripple-Brim Hat demands a **SweetHeart Soap** *Complexion*

Now hats are smaller and smarter! This fall your hair's cut shorter, your hat fits snugly—to give your head that new, neat look that's so Parisian.

So change to SweetHeart's 1-2-3 Extra Lather Beauty Care

It's a fashion frame-up to dramatize *you!* See how the ripple brim of this stunning new hat makes *your* face the picture. That's why soft, clear, radiant skin is a necessity.

So be smart about your beauty care. Be done with inadequate cleansing. Awaken your complexion's true loveliness the famous SweetHeart way. For one minute night and morning, massage your face with SweetHeart Soap's *extra*

lather. Rinse with warm, then icy cold water. Now see these 3 glorious results—your skin is (1) *cleansed* (2) *stimulated* (3) *brightened!* Your beauty blooms.

For this 3-way beauty help, insist on SweetHeart Soap. SweetHeart gives up to *twice as much lather* as the average beauty soap. The rich, creamy, abundant lather you want for these basic steps to clearer, fresher, more alluring skin.

The soap that AGREES with your skin

DON'T WASTE SOAP
It contains vital materials.

Congressman Carroll B. Reece, of Tennessee, takes over as chairman of the Republican National Committee, formerly held by Herbert Brownell.

A proud Mrs. Reece congratulates her husband on his new appointment.

Mary Pickford,
America's First Lady of Film, receives a royal welcome on her arrival in London.

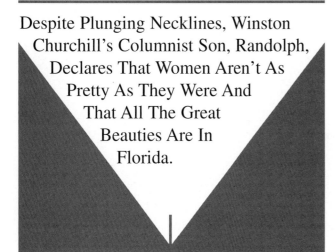

THE NEW GREY MARES AIN'T WHAT THEY USED TO BE

Despite Plunging Necklines, Winston Churchill's Columnist Son, Randolph, Declares That Women Aren't As Pretty As They Were And That All The Great Beauties Are In Florida.

Magazine Illustrators Dub Mrs. Elliot Roosevelt As Being Among Those Having The Most Kissable Lips In America.

* Gertrude Stein Greets U.S. Writer, Richard Wright ("Native Son," "Black Boy") On His Arrival In Paris As A Cultural Guest Of The French Government.

* Eva Peron Buys A $30,000 Carpet For The Presidential Home.

* The American Museum Of Natural History Adds A Sculpture Of Joe Louis' Right Fist To Its Comparative Anatomy Collection.

* World War I Hero, Alvin York, Strikes Oil Near His Home In Tennessee's Cumberland Mountains.

* Laurence Olivier And His Wife, Vivien Leigh, Make A Safe Crash Landing In The Connecticut Countryside After Their Plane Loses An Engine.

* George Bernard Shaw, The World's Greatest Living Literary Figure, Turns 90.

* Beautiful Hollywood Star, Linda Christian Sentenced To Five Days In Jail For Speeding.

* During A Radio Interview, Eleanor Roosevelt Says She Deplores Attempts To Make Men And Women Equal Instead Of Complementing Each Other.

* Eleanor Roosevelt Badly Bruised In Three-Car Collision After Falling Asleep At The Wheel Of Her New Lincoln Sedan.

COUPLING

John Huston & Evelyn Keyes

Prince Louis II (Ruler of Monaco) & Ghyslaine Domanget

Kitty Carlisle & Moss Hart

George Balanchine & Maria Tallchief

UNCOUPLING

Celeste Holm & A. Schuyler Dunning

Joe E. Lewis & Martha Stewart

George Abbott & Mary Sinclair

Boris Karloff & Evelyn Helmore

Joan Fontaine & William Dozier

Freddie Bartholomew & Maely Daniele

John Wayne & Esperanza Baur

Mervyn LeRoy & Kathryn Prest Byfield Spiegel

Elizabeth de Gaulle & Alain de Boissieu

Myrna Loy & Gene Markey

Artie Shaw & Kathleen Winsor

Olivia de Havilland & Marcus Goodrich

Cornelius Vanderbilt & Maria Feliza Pablus

Diana Barrymore & Bramwell Fletcher

Ann Sothern & Robert Sterling

Diana Barrymore & Bramwell Fletcher

Joan Crawford & Philip Terry

Jascha Heifetz & Florence Vidor Heifetz

Artie Shaw & Ava Gardner

Ann Dvorak & Leslie Fenton

George Vanderbilt & Lucille Parsons Vanderbilt

Oscar Homolka & Florence Meyer Homolka

Stirling Hayden & Madeleine Carroll

GRIEVOUS AND IRRECONCILABLE DIFFERENCES OH YOU CAD!

Gloria Swanson Sues Her Fifth Husband For Support On The Grounds That:

• He drinks too much;

• She prefers living in her apartment on Fifth Avenue, but he wants to live at his place on Park Avenue;

• He prefers sleeping in an oversized bed, while she prefers twin beds;

• He never built the glass bathroom on their yacht.

How much does she want to be compensated for this dastardly behavior? $1,000 weekly to be exact!

WHAT A YEAR IT WAS!

1946 ADVERTISEMENT

You're so smart...

You always have the perfect answer.
For these smart watch bands by
Jacques Kreisler write their own daily themes
on what the educated wrist will wear.
Beautifully gold-finished in enduring
Kreisler quality, they go to the head of every
class in this season's back-to-school parade.

For men: A. Kreisler Basketweave
Watch Band, 12.50.
B. Kreisler Domeflex Expansion
Watch Band, Stainless Back, 9.95.
For women: C. Lady Thinflex Expansion
Watch Bracelet, Stainless Back, 8.95.
D. Basketweave Watch Bracelet, 8.95.
Prices include Federal Tax.

At Fine Stores Everywhere

Jacques Kreisler

WORLD'S LARGEST MAKER OF JEWELRY WATCH BANDS FOR MEN AND WOMEN

31

1946

"WINNIE" RECEIVES WARM WELCOME IN NEW YORK

One of the original Big Three, Britain's former Prime Minister, Winston Spencer Churchill arrives in New York to deliver an important speech.

Newly-elected Mayor O'Dwyer greets Mr. Churchill, the man who led England to victory.

WHAT A YEAR IT WAS!

Dissenters gathered at City Hall are quickly subdued.

Speaking at an official dinner before a distinguished audience of 2,000, Mr. Churchill backs up his position that he does not believe that Russian rulers wish for war at the present time and that war is not inevitable or imminent.

1946 CHURCHILL GOES TO MIAMI

Winston Churchill arrives in Miami for a well-earned 6-week vacation.

The former Prime Minister is a guest at the home of a friend in Miami Beach.

Mr. Churchill, accompanied by his wife, is host to a press conference during which he warns against too rapid a drift toward world collectivism.

New York's Postmaster, Albert Goldman, Personally Answers And Distributes Donated Gifts To The Neediest From The More Than 10,000 Letters Addressed To Santa Claus Each Christmas.

•

Movie Star Van Johnson Receives Fan Mail Mostly From Older Women Who Want To Play Matchmaker.

•

President Truman's Favorite Dinner: Steak And Baked Potato.

Actress June Knight Finally Receives Telephone After A Year's Wait And Sends Out "New Arrival" Announcements With Date, Time And Weight.

•

Former Barber, Perry Como, Cuts His Young Son's Hair.

•

John F. Kennedy Runs For First Political Office And Wins Election To The House By 78,000 Votes.

FOR I ONLY HAVE DOTS FOR YOU...

When "The Polka Dot Girl" Chili Williams Was Seen Dotless In Public, William Schiller, Known As "The Polka Dot King" Promptly Sued Her For Breach Of Contract Stating That Under The Terms Of Their Agreement She Is Required To Wear Nothing But Polka Dots.

COME TO ME MY MELON-COD-DE BABY...

A sardine fisherman by the name of Vincent Sallecito was doing a day's work as an extra in a film being shot in Monterey Bay starring Greer Garson. A huge wave knocked the beautiful Miss Garson off of the rock on which she was sitting at which point the gallant Mr. Sallecito jumped in immediately and carried her to safety. Miss Garson was treated for cuts, bruises, and a sprained back at a local hospital while the fisherman had his moment of fame and a chance to hold one of the most beautiful women in America.

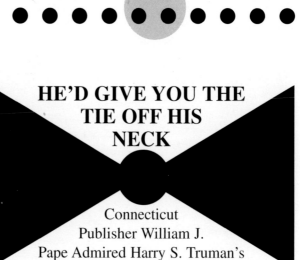

HE'D GIVE YOU THE TIE OFF HIS NECK

Connecticut Publisher William J. Pape Admired Harry S. Truman's Silver-Streaked Black Bow Tie Who Loaned It To Him For An Evening.

1946

Jackie Cooper Returns Home After Serving A 26-Month Stint In The Navy.

Charles "Lucky" Luciano Sings His Way Out Of His 10-20 Year Sentence By Providing The United States With Information On Italy During The War And His Reward Is Deportation To The Old Country.

☞ Jean-Paul Sartre, Novelist, Playwright, Essayist, Prophet And Author Of The Bible On Existentialism, *"Being and Nothingness,"* Arrives In New York For Lecture Tour Including Engagements At Yale, Harvard and Princeton.

☞ George Bernard Shaw's Solution To Overpopulation: Every Woman Should Be Paid $8,000 By Her Man Before Bearing His Child.

☞ British Historian Arnold J. Toynbee Receives A $152,000 Grant From The Rockefeller Foundation To Write A World War II History Of International Relations.

☞ Haile Selassie Receives The Wendell L. Willkie Memorial Award From The Manhattan Based African Academy Of Arts And Research For His Contribution To International Peace And Good Will.

☞ Dr. Lise Meitner, Refugee German Physicist And Pioneer Contributor To The Atomic Bomb Is Chosen "Woman Of The Year" By The Women's National Press Club.

Franklin D. Roosevelt's Stamp Collection Auctioned Off At New York Gallery.

WHAT A YEAR IT WAS!

"you bet I'm particular!
...I want my sodas in

"What I mean is—at fountains or other public places I don't like drinking out of something that another person has already used. An individual Dixie Cup has never touched any lips but mine. Take this soda...it *tastes* better in a Dixie Cup because you know it's *clean*."

1946

Guy Lombardo Wins National Motorboat Sweepstakes In Red Bank, New Jersey Competition.

The International Sound Research Institute Gives Annual Award For Good Diction To Ingrid Bergman.

Playwright Thorton Wilder Is Made Member Of The Order Of The British Empire In Manhattan For His Help In Planning Combined Operations In The Mediterranean.

General Douglas MacArthur Receives The French Grand Cross Of The Legion Of Honor In Tokyo.

Mother Frances Cabrini, Founder Of The Order Of The Sacred Heart And America's First Saint, Is Canonized In

The Vatican Elevates New York's Francis Spellman To Cardinal.

SOMEONE'S IN THE KITCHEN WITH BESSIE

First Lady, Bess Truman, And Some Of Her Friends Don Aprons And Whip Up A Meal In The White House Kitchen for 70 Students Of The First Lady's Spanish Teacher.

Frank Sinatra And Ingrid Bergman Voted Least Cooperative Stars By Hollywood Newspaperwomen With Betty Grable And Ginger Rogers Tying For Second Place.

WHAT A YEAR IT WAS!

Shirley Temple's Brother, George, Wins First Match In His Wrestling Debut.

SOMETHING OLD, SOMETHING NEW, SOMETHING BORROWED...ER...LET'S SKIP RIGHT TO SOMETHING BLUE

Newlywed Shirley Temple Turns Down Fan's Request To Borrow Her Wedding Gown, Stating That Some Things Have To Remain Personal And Sentimental.

HERE HE IS, MR. AMERICA

Alan Stephan, Ex-Sailor From Cicero, Illinois, Is Voted Mr. America.

The Miss United Nations Title Goes To Marjorie Bertha Morgenstierne, Daughter Of Norwegian Ambassador Wilhelm.

Most Glamorous Mothers In America

RITA HAYWORTH
&
LANA TURNER

PRINCESS ELIZABETH, HEIRESS TO BRITAIN'S THRONE, AND GREEK PRINCE PHILIP ENGAGED BUT WEDDING PLANS DELAYED BY KING GEORGE VI DUE TO POLITICAL SITUATION IN ATHENS.

Passings

JIMMY WALKER, Mr. New York, Dies At 65.

WHY DO AMERICAN GIRLS RATE FIRST FOR CHARM?

Take-it-easy clothes. Skylarking comfort —that's for you! Easy-shouldered suits, good-to-walk-in shoes. And comfort-insurance for "difficult" days. So, the smart gals choose the sanitary napkin that's *first* for softness—Modess! 3 out of 4 voted it *softer* to the touch, in a nation poll.

Social Security. Poise? You've plenty! Growing up with boys, dancing lessons, have taught you how to forget yourself, have *fun!* Poise-polisher—the napkin that's *first for safety!* Hospital-tested Modess, which 209 nurses found less likely to strike through than leading layer-type napkins.

That scrubbed look. Scads of soap-and-water—every day! You're spring-breeze dainty in every detail! So again it's Modess

for you. *First* napkin to bring you this priceless daintiness aid—a unique, triple-proved *deodorant* sealed right in.

Those artful extras. You're a smoothie with the powder puff, lipstick brush—all the "pluses" of super-grooming. And when it comes to comfort-extras, at no extra cost—

Modess gives them to you. *And does it first!* No wonder more and more girls are saying, "I'll take Modess!" Box of 12, full-size or Junior size, only 22¢.

First for softness
MODESS

The carrier Franklin D. Roosevelt, the mightiest warship afloat, makes her initial shakedown cruise. This 45-ton vessel was commissioned on Navy Day in honor of the late president.

She carries a nest of planes protected by gun batteries that were unheard of before the FDR was built.

The signal officer still plays a key role in bringing the Corsairs to safety.

NAVY TESTS NEW PLANE

The Navy tests newest post-war addition to its aerial defense weapons—the Douglas BT-2-D, a combination torpedo and dive bomber.

With a 2,500 horsepower engine and a cruising range of 1,500 miles, the latest weapon of defense is equipped with new diving brakes that slow it down to landing speed in seconds.

The Civil Aeronautics Authority Predicts That By 1955 One Family In 100 Will Own Its Own Plane.

Jet-Propelled Fighter Plane Sets Nonstop Transcontinental Speed Record Flying From Long Beach, California To La Guardia Field In 4 Hours 13 Minutes.

A Spokesman For The Agriculture Department Reveals The Development Of A Radio Proximity Fuse Which Will Allow Fire Fighters To Fight Forest Fires In The Future With Water Bombs Dropped From Large Bombers.

WHAT A YEAR IT WAS!

SLEEPING HABITS INTERPRETED

On Your Back ....Fearless
Stomach ....Intense
Curled Up ....Escapist
Hugging Your Pillow ...Need Affection
Talk In Your Sleep .....Talk Too Much When Awake

Bell Telephone Predicts Long Distance Calls Will Be Processed As Quickly As Local Calls Within The Next 10 Years.

U. S. Post Office Predicts Speedy Future Airmail Service Through Use Of "Flying Mailcar" —Converted World War II "Flying Boxcars" Where Mail Would Be Sorted While In Flight.

Britain's Famed Physicist, Sir Edward Appleton, Predicts That Some Day The Mountains Of The Moon May Be Accurately Charted By Radar.

The Addition Of Bright Colors In Industrial Plants Seen As One Way Of Cutting Down On Accidents.

FAVORITE COLORS OF AMERICAN MEN
1. Blue
2. Red
3. Purple
4. Green
5. Orange
6. Yellow

Rear Admiral Byrd Heads South Pole Expedition Involving 4,000 Men And A Dozen Vessels.

New Cloud Meter Developed By General Electric May Allow Weather Forecasts Of The Future To Predict Amount Of Expected Rainfall.

1946

A BIG DAY FOR DOGS AT THE WESTMINSTER DOG SHOW HELD AT NEW YORK'S MADISON SQUARE GARDEN

Proud owners show off their prized canines.

A dog in a hat is worth two on a leash?

And the champion is "Hetherington Model Rhythm," first Fox Terrier to win the Kennel Club's top prize since 1937.

Blessed with the best weather in 11 years, 75,000 people march up New York's Fifth Avenue in the annual St. Patrick's Day Parade.

The famous old 69th, the Fighting Irish, who distinguished themselves again in the last war, add a military note to the peace-time event.

THE LUCK OF THE IRISH

Among the more than a million and a half people watching the parade are the bishops (right) representing Cardinal Spellman, and Irish born and bred Mayor O'Dwyer and movie actor Pat O'Brien (left).

President Truman Approves $2.4 Billion Bill For G.I. Leave Pay

I'M SO HUNGRY, I COULD EAT A HORSE...*AND DID!*

With the soaring price of meat making beef too expensive, New Yorkers have gotten on their high horse and have turned to eating Trigger's brothers and sisters. While former Mayor LaGuardia denounces this trend as being a sign of degeneration, Health Commissioner Weinstein states that horse meat is as nutritious and as good as any other meat.

With The Ending Of The War, Industrial Workers Have Less Incidences Of Indigestion, Insomnia, Fatigue, High Blood Pressure And Nervous Exhaustion.

THE COST OF WORLD WAR II: $680,000,000,000

North Hollywood Pharmacy Calls Police To Handle Mob Who Snatch Up 2,000 Pieces Of Post-War Bubble Gum In Two Hours.

LOOK OUT OIL OF OLAY

The United States Department Of Agriculture Announces The Breeding Of Two Species Of Wrinkle-Free Sheep.

The Lord Mayor Of Bristol, Britain Welcomes The Banana Boat Tilapa Which Brings The First Bananas To Britain After Five Years.

Marines Land On Alcatraz To Quell Attempted Jail Break.

EASTER
SUNDAY
APRIL 21ST

The season's most popular messenger

Remember her on Easter with a Whitman's Sampler. She'll be the proudest lady . . . proud of your thoughtfulness in remembering her and remembering the day . . . proud, too, of your excellent taste in choosing her dream candy, the chocolates every woman knows are America's finest.

CRISP ALMONDS covered in thick, dark gleaming chocolate . . . a rich delight to bite into. One of the many taste thrills in your Sampler.

Whitman's
CHOCOLATES

A WOMAN NEVER FORGETS THE MAN WHO REMEMBERS

48

WANNA GET MARRIED?

HERE'S THE IDEAL QUALITIES TO LOOK FOR IN A MATE

The HUSBAND

Ambitious
Aware Of Social Problems
Common Interests
Considerate
Dependable
Desire For Children
Educated
Financially Secure
Good Character
Good Companion
Mentally & Physically Fit
Pressed Clothes
Religious Beliefs
Self-Assured
Sense Of Humor
Shined Shoes
Sincere
Supportive
Thoughtful
Tolerant
Trustworthy

The WIFE

Ages Gracefully
Cheerful
Combination Wife, Sweetheart & Mistress
Doesn't Make A Man Feel Married
Economical Dresser
Good Listener
Honest
Intelligent (But Not Smarter Than Her Husband)
Mutual Interests
Never Wears Bobby Socks
Sense Of Humor & Ability To Laugh At Herself
Unaffected

FROM "I DO" TO "I DON'T"

With more than 800,000 out of a total of 1,500,000 American war-wed GI's back in the States, the divorce rate has sky-rocketed with one out of every four of these often-times hasty marriages ending. Experts predict that two out of three wartime marriages will end in divorce by 1950.

A Woman In Camden, New Jersey, Is Granted A Divorce On The Grounds That Her Husband Made Her Duck Under The Dashboard Whenever He Drove Past A Girlfriend.

And In Salem, Massachusetts A Woman Sued For Divorce On The Grounds That Her Husband Was Too Affectionate And Stayed Home Too Much.

Navy Unveils Wartime Aerial TV Camera

An aerial television camera is loaded into a plane for a series of tests.

The flying eye photographs and transmits its pictures of targets and objectives up to 200 miles away by one of the most compact transmitters yet developed.

At a television room 40 miles away the images take shape on the screen, the kind of information that led to the sinking of Japanese ships in the Pacific.

1946

EINSTEIN SPEAKS OUT ON WORLD SURVIVAL

◆ We must abandon competition and secure cooperation vs. increasing size of armies.

◆ We cannot prepare for war at the same time we prepare for a world community.

◆ As long as we make bombs, we are also making hate and suspicion.

◆ Not even scientists completely understand atomic energy and the ultimate destructive capabilities of the bomb.

◆ The Emergency Committee of Atomic Scientists in Princeton, New Jersey was formed to disseminate information to the public as although science created this clear danger, the real problem is in the minds and hearts of men.

◆ We must realize that we cannot simultaneously plan for both war and peace.

◆ When we are clear in heart and mind—only then shall we find courage to surmount the fear which haunts the world.

Second Underwater Atomic Explosion At Bikini Sinks 10 Ships Including Battleship "Arkansas" And Carrier "Saratoga."

Albert Einstein Expresses Regret Over Use Of The Atom Bomb On Hiroshima.

Industrial Use Of Atomic Energy Explored.

Captain Eddie Rickenbacker Suggests An Atomic Bomb Be Dropped On The 1,800 Ft. Thick Antarctic Polar Icecap To Crack It Open.

WHAT A YEAR IT WAS!

THE AIR FORCE GETS READY FOR ATOM BOMB TESTS AT BIKINI

Radio crews man ground instruments which send big flying forts into the air without pilots.

For the first time in history a crewless four-engine plane is handled by remote radio control.

Destined for Bikini Atoll, a palm-studded island in the Marshall Islands, the battle-scarred B-17's are considered expendable.

THE AIR FORCE GETS READY FOR ATOM BOMB TESTS AT BIKINI

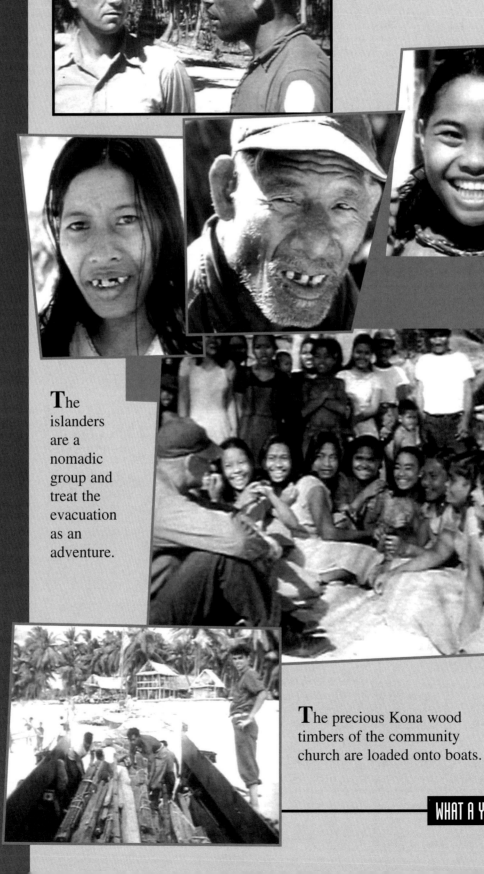

American officials discuss evacuation plans with the natives.

The islanders are a nomadic group and treat the evacuation as an adventure.

The precious Kona wood timbers of the community church are loaded onto boats.

WHAT A YEAR IT WAS!

Building materials including leaves for roofing are loaded onto boats along with personal belongings.

The women wave goodbye to their men who will return to get them after they build their new homes 109 miles away.

The Mayor Of Anchorage, Alaska Issues An Edict That Any Man Seen Without A Beard During The City's Fur Carnival Period Will Be Charged With Indecent Exposure.

The Average American Woman Spends Less Than $4.00 Yearly On Hats And Every Five Years Consumes Her Height In Lipstick.

Jitterbug Dancing Banned In A Ballroom In Sioux City, Iowa Due To Objections Over Bumps, Kicks And Jumps.

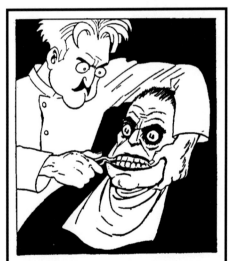

Metropolitan Life Insurance Company Reveals More Fatal Accidents Among Adults Occur In The Bedroom Than Any Other Room In The House.

According To Dental Authorities, The Majority Of Americans Don't Brush Their Teeth Regularly And Don't Even Own Toothbrushes.

Did you know that in Denver, a woman can't be photographed in a bathing suit without her permission and in England, it's against the law to marry your mother-in-law.

Meet Mohara...for <u>daylong</u> crisp appearance

First impressions count at any time of the year...never more so than in summer. Hot weather may be an alibi, but no longer an excuse for sloppy appearance. Now, smart grooming is easy, lasting and economical with the right fabric in your summer suit.

Through a most careful blending, Pacific has developed Mohara, a new, pleasantly cool tropical plus. Mohara combines all the natural advantages of worsted with mohair, the most resilient and lustrous of all animal fibres. There

is added richness in Mohara's luxurious sheen...greater beauty in Mohara's silky, crisp appearance...longer staying power in Mohara's shape and crease retention...more wilt resistance to heat and humidity for daylong freshness ...plus colors that cool (determined by infra-red reflectance tests).

Joseph & Feiss' skilled tailoring has fashioned all these marvels of the fabric into suits that help you enjoy summer living at its cool, presentable best. Pacific Mills, Worsted Division, 261 Fifth Avenue, New York 16.

Available in limited but growing quantities at leading **$32**
stores from coast to coast, single and double-breasted models

For further information write to the Joseph & Feiss Co., Cleveland 1, Ohio; or Pacific Mills, Worsted Division, Retail Service Bureau, 200 Fifth Avenue, New York 10.

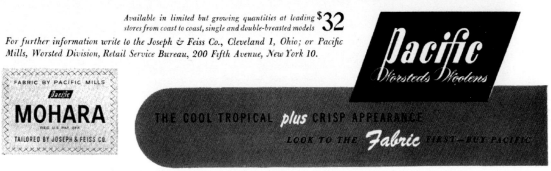

FABRIC BY PACIFIC MILLS
Pacific
MOHARA
REG. U.S. PAT. OFF.
TAILORED BY JOSEPH & FEISS CO.

Pacific
Worsteds Woolens

THE COOL TROPICAL *plus* CRISP APPEARANCE

LOOK TO THE Fabric FIRST—BUY PACIFIC

Happy Felton demonstrates acceptable dunking practices with his hide-and-dunk *(left)* and donut-on-a-string *(right)*.

Some of his friends are for a more traditional approach of the straight dunk-and-bite method.

This dunker has developed the two-fisted dunk-and-bite approach guaranteed to double your dunking pleasure.

Liverpool, England Shipping Center Fights Series Of Unexplained Fires– Sabotage Suspected

German warship, captured by the British Navy, is latest of five vessels destroyed by fires of unknown origin.

Despite valiant fire-fighting efforts, this 17,000 ton craft destined to serve as a British troop ship becomes a gutted and charred wreck.

According To An Article Published By The Population Reference Bureau, With The More Educated Sector Of The Population Having Less Children, The World Will Face A Shortage Of Brain Power.

Senator J. William Fulbright, Ex-Rhodes Scholar, Initiates Grants For Overseas Academic Exchange.

According To The U.S. Bureau Of The Census, Families Where The Wife Attended College Have Fewer Children.

The Bureau Of The Census Releases Figures Showing That Women Born In America To Foreign Or To A Combination Of Foreign And American Parents Not Only Marry At A Later Age Than Those Of American Descent But Are Less Likely To Marry At All.

EDUCATORS AGREE THAT A THIRD OF ALL HIGH SCHOOL STUDENTS CAN'T READ OR WRITE WELL ENOUGH TO LEARN FROM TEXT BOOKS.

10,000,000 AMERICAN ADULTS REPORTED ILLITERATE ACCORDING TO STUDY CONDUCTED AT NEW YORK UNIVERSITY.

WHAT PRICE FAME & GLORY?

According to a report in THE AMERICAN SOCIOLOGICAL REVIEW, Americans who achieve great enough prominence to be listed in WHO'S WHO are less likely to live as long as their unfamous contemporaries.

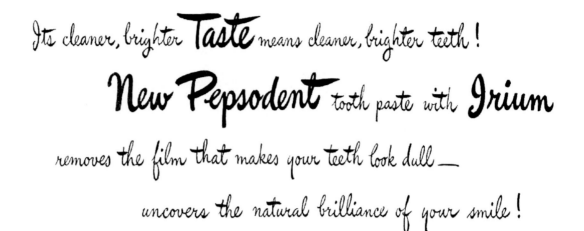

U.S. Treasury Marks 15th Anniversary of Series E Bond

Jeff Chandler makes a pitch for investing in government bonds.

COUPLINGS & UNCOUPLINGS

MARRIAGES . .2,291,000
DIVORCES . . .610,000

ARRIVALS

BIRTHS 3,411,000

U.S. Birthrates Soar As Servicemen Return.

LIFE EXPECTANCY FOR 1946 BIRTHS: Three Out Of Four Will Reach Age 57.

The **LONG** And The ꜱʜᴏʀᴛ Of It

Height Of Average Woman: 5' 3 1/4"
Weight: 127 Lbs.

Height Of Average Man: 5' 8 3/4"
Weight: 153 1/2 Lbs.

WHAT A YEAR IT WAS!

DIVERS PUT ON SHOW FOR WOUNDED VETS AT FLORIDA ARMY HOSPITAL

Divers go into action on a greased pole making it "Operation Slippery."

A development of
B.F.Goodrich
FIRST IN RUBBER

For one truck tire: take 16 miles of rayon cord . . .

A typical example of B. F. Goodrich improvement in tires

THE backbone of every truck tire is the cord fabric. That's what takes the wallops. It's when the cords begin to pop that a blow-out is in the making.

Ordinary tire fabric is woven with small threads criss-crossing the cords. With this process the cords cannot be absolutely straight and parallel. Cords which are too tight carry more than their share of the load, often break.

B.F.Goodrich engineers developed a method for making rayon cord fabric without any cross threads!

Each cord as it comes from the spool is kept under even tension, evenly spaced with as many as 36 cords to the inch. They are then dipped in adhesive and covered with rubber which holds them permanently in place. Cords can't touch each other. And because of a special tension regulating device there are no loose cords, no tight cords. All are under the same tension.

In just one 10.00-20 truck tire there are 16 miles of this rayon cord — cord carefully controlled as to stretch, moisture content, and tension.

The use of this rayon cord, without cross threads, and with controlled tension, results in truck tires of uniform strength; tires less susceptible to bruises,

blow-outs, and cracking. Tire mileage is increased.

It's a typical development of B.F.Goodrich continuing research — research that improves tires for every purpose. *The B.F.Goodrich Company, Akron, Ohio.*

Truck Tires BY

B.F. Goodrich

Representatives from all faiths meet for National Brotherhood Week.

Former Governor Patton, Chairman, makes a plea for tolerance stating:

"It should be repeated time and again that anyone who lights the flame of bigotry or intolerance in America lights a fire underneath his own home."

National School Lunch Act Becomes Law.

3,200 Protestant And Jewish Clergymen Representing Every State In The Union Endorse Planned Parenthood Services As A "Fundamental Democratic Right."

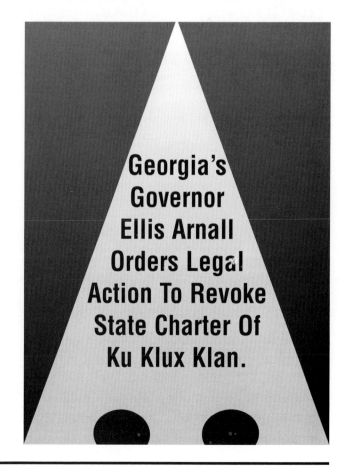

Georgia's Governor Ellis Arnall Orders Legal Action To Revoke State Charter Of Ku Klux Klan.

Variety

Celebrates Its 40th Birthday.

LIFE

Magazine Celebrates Its Tenth Anniversary.

Der Spiegel

Begins Publication In Hamburg.

The United Nations Educational, Scientific And Cultural Organization (UNESCO) Is Created.

The Statue Of Liberty Celebrates Her 60th Birthday.

Mexico City Builds The World's Largest, Most Modern Bull Ring.

First **CARE** Packages Arrive In France.

Pennsylvania Railroad Celebrates A Century Of Service To The American People.

- London's Heathrow Airport Formally Opens. Transatlantic Passenger Service To North America Begins Mid-Year.

- Shuttle Bus Service To Parking Facilities Begins In Chicago.

WHAT A YEAR IT WAS!

will be to see the folks who make those delightful *Borden's Fine Cheeses.*"

"Cheese!" drooled Elmer. "Why didn't you say so before? If I went along, do you suppose they'd let me do a little sampling on the side?"

"May-bee," doubtfully considered Elsie. "But, you know, Borden's has its own staff of cheese tasters and testers, men who have devoted lifetimes to creating grand cheese foods like Borden's Chateau—that's the one with the exciting, tangy Cheddar flavor. It's—"

CREAM IN EVERY VITAMIN-RICH SIP OF BORDEN'S HOMOGENIZED MILK!

"Quit it!" begged Elmer. "You're driving me crazy."

"You're not the only one," laughed Elsie, "who goes crazy about the wonderful foods Borden's makes. Folks all over the country, and up in Canada, too, certainly love them. They buy them, and buy them, and buy them again, year after year. All of which proves, dear, that quality counts."

"Quality—my eye!" argued Elmer. "It's *taste* that counts."

"But, dear, you can *taste* quality," soothed Elsie. "You taste it in every delicious, smooth sip of glorious *Borden's Homogenized Milk.* There's Vitamin D in every drop, you know. And every little globule of

GREAT TREATS ANY TIME BORDEN'S ICE CREAM AND MILK SHERBETS!

"But, darling, I'm going away <u>because</u> I love you!" cried Elsie

"D<small>ON'T PULL</small> that old one on me," roared Elmer, the bull. "That's the same line you hand me every time you want to get your own way—and I'm not having any! What I want to know, woman, is where you're headed for and *why.*"

"And I'll be delighted to tell you," cheerfully chirped Elsie, the Borden Cow. "I'm off on a flying tour of Borden's plants and laboratories."

"That's a hot one," haw-hawed Elmer. "And what in Cowdom Come will *you* do in a laboratory?"

"Oh, I won't *do* anything," answered Elsie. "I'm just going to watch my friends, the Borden scientists, do things. Dear, it's better than a magic show!"

"What! No rabbits?" sneered Elmer.

"Of course they have rabbits—in the *testing* labora-

HEMO HAS A NEW AND WONDERFUL "MILK-CHOCOLATE" FLAVOR!

tories for work on vitamins," smiled Elsie. "And speaking of vitamins, you'd be entranced with the *Hemo* plant! You could see how vitamins and minerals everyone needs every day are blended into a glorious *milk-chocolate* flavored drink. You could get a first-hand idea of vitamin control, too, when the scientists assay Hemo. You—"

"*Assay!*" exclaimed Elmer suspiciously. "What kind of foreign talk is that?"

"It's not just talk, dear," explained Elsie. "It's a very, very serious scientific procedure. A sort of check and double check on vitamin content. You know, the Borden folks are mighty particular about making everything as good as they say it is. For instance, when

MAKE GRAND SOUPS WITH BORDEN'S EVAPORATED MILK!

they say *Borden's Evaporated Milk* is rich in Vitamin D, you can bet your bottom dollar they're right—400 units per reconstituted quart! . . . Yes, dear, Borden's controls every single step in the preparation of its wonderful foods!"

"One thing they'll never control," groaned Elmer,

EXTRA-NOURISHING EXTRA-SAVORY BORDEN'S FINE CHEESES!

"and that's your tongue. Maybe *you* can control it long enough to tell me *exactly* where you're going?"

"Of course, dear," answered Elsie. "My first stop

cream is broken into tiny particles and spread all through the milk."

"No matter how you spread it," sighed Elmer, "it's still Borden's. Woman, woman, can't you ever even *think* of anything but business?"

"Of course, dear," brightly twittered Elsie. "I *love* to think of fun and good times, too. And when I do, I think of *Borden's Ice Cream and Milk Sherbets.* They really make a party a *party.* And they're such good, nourishing treats *any* time."

"Any time, every time, *all* the time," wearily mumbled Elmer, "it's Borden's, Borden's, Borden's."

"Why, dear, you made a slogan!" enthused Elsie. "Almost as nice as our famous one—*if it's Borden's, it's GOT to be good!*"

- if it's Borden's. it's <u>got</u> to be good!

TUNE IN **GINNY SIMMS** IN A **GREAT RADIO SHOW** WITH **Comedy Guest Stars** FRIDAY EVENINGS - CBS

© The Borden Company

END OF THE RAINBOW

Thousands of people showed up to say goodbye to the famous Rainbow Club in London, a Red Cross club that entertained 18 million GI's during the war.

Distinguished guest Eleanor Roosevelt, addressing the sentimental gathering, said:

"It is a sad day for many, because partings are always sad. But it is a joyous day too. The war is over, and men who came here for the war can now go home."

So the last dance is danced at this favorite wartime rendezvous.

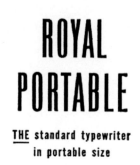

ICE CREAM

Americans Consume A Record 714 Million Gallons Of Ice Cream.

☆ According To The "AMERICAN FRUIT GROWER" The Banana Is A Berry But The Strawberry Is Just A Fruit.

☆ New York Christmas Shoppers Overrun Macy's And Gimbels' In Biggest Buying Spree In History.

Constant Bombardment Of Street Noises Thought To Be The Cause Of The Shrill, High-Pitched Voice Of The Average New Yorker.

GREAT BRITAIN LAUNCHES "GREENBELT" PROGRAM WHICH IS DESIGNED TO CREATE GARDEN SETTINGS WITHIN THE CITIES.

Dutch Windmills Dwindle To 1,400—Down From 9,000 In The 1870's.

Murder Incorporated Hit Man "Bugsy" Siegel Builds The Flamingo Hotel In Las Vegas, Launching The Desert Town Into A Gambling Resort.

Brooklyn's Famed Coney Island Attracts As Many As One Million People On An Average Sunday Who Stroll The Widest Boardwalk In The World And Who Lose And Find Approximately 2,200 Children A Season.

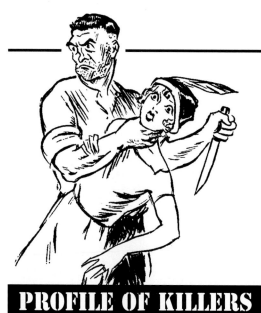

PROFILE OF KILLERS

Older men who murder women usually do so to avenge acts of infidelity or unrequited love while younger men are more likely to kill other men instead of women and usually commit the crime during an argument.

How Many Miles Of Thread Does It Take To Dress A Man?

ITEM OF CLOTHING	NO. MILES OF THREAD
Underwear	9
Socks	2 1/2
Shirt	10
Tie	1
Suit	36

TOTAL MILES OF THREAD: 58 1/2 MILES

New York Issues Record Number Of Marriage Licenses With Most Of The Prospective Grooms Wearing Discharge Buttons In Their Lapels.

MISS AMERICA:
Marilyn Buferd
(Los Angeles, California)

PASSINGS

PATTY SMITH HILL, Progressive Education Expert, Author Of The Verse "Happy Birthday," Dies At 78.

DR. FREDERICK L. HOFFMAN, Founder Of The American Cancer Society, Dies At 80.

72

BUSINESS

Department Of Agriculture Orders U.S. Bakers To Reduce Size Of Bread Loaves And Rolls.

- Walter Reuther Elected President Of United Automobile Workers.

- Conviction Of Three U.S. Tobacco Companies For Violation Of Antitrust Act Upheld By The U.S. Supreme Court.

- Sharp Rise in Butter Prices Seen After U.S. Government Ends Its Subsidy.

- The Dow-Jones Industrial Average Reaches Post-1929 High Of 212.50 But Falls To 163.12.

President Truman Ends All Wage, Price And Salary Controls Exempting Rent Ceilings, Sugar and Rice.

U.S. Farm Prices Reach Highest Level Since 1920.

A & P Food Chain Convicted Of Monopoly Acts.

1946

MEAT PACKERS STRIKE PARALYZES NATION'S MEAT SUPPLY

More than a quarter million packing house workers strike across the nation for higher wages.

Negotiations between union, government and packing officials fail to produce an agreement, forcing the government to step in and take over.

The formal seizure notice is posted and union leaders order the strikers back to work.

The American flag is raised over seized plants and assembly lines in slaughter-houses begin full operations.

WHAT A YEAR IT WAS!

1946

WORST WORK STOPPAGE SINCE 1919 SWEEPS THE UNITED STATES

JANUARY

7,000 Western Union Workers Walk Off Job, Paralyzing Telegraph Services In New York.

200,000 Members Of United Electrical Radio And Machine Workers Of America Walk Off Jobs In 16 States Halting Production Of All Appliances.

800,000 Pittsburgh Steel Workers Join Millions On Strike.

FEBRUARY

Mayor O'Dwyer Declares State Of Emergency As Striking Tugboat Workers Cripple New York.

10,000 Striking Philadelphia Transit Employees Paralyze City Transportation.

WHAT A YEAR IT WAS!

FEBRUARY / MARCH

STRIKE SETTLEMENTS REACHED AT FORD, GENERAL MOTORS AND GENERAL ELECTRIC.

APRIL

Approximately 400,000 Soft Coal Miners Strike.

MAY

U.S. Government Seizes Railroads To Avert Strike Which Commences Anyway.

John L. Lewis Settles 45-Day Coal Strike In White House Negotiations.

SEPTEMBER

Truck Strike Hits New York, Curtailing Deliveries Of Food.

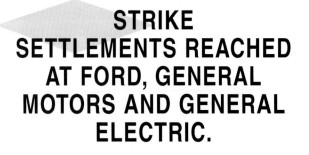

Shipping Stops On All Coasts As Worst Maritime Strike In History Hits The U.S.

OCTOBER

First Strike In Airline History Staged By 1,400 Pilots And Co-Pilots Of Transcontinental And Western Air, Inc.

DECEMBER

U.S. Government Indicts John L. Lewis For Contempt And Fines Him $10,000 And United Mine Workers $3.5 Million.

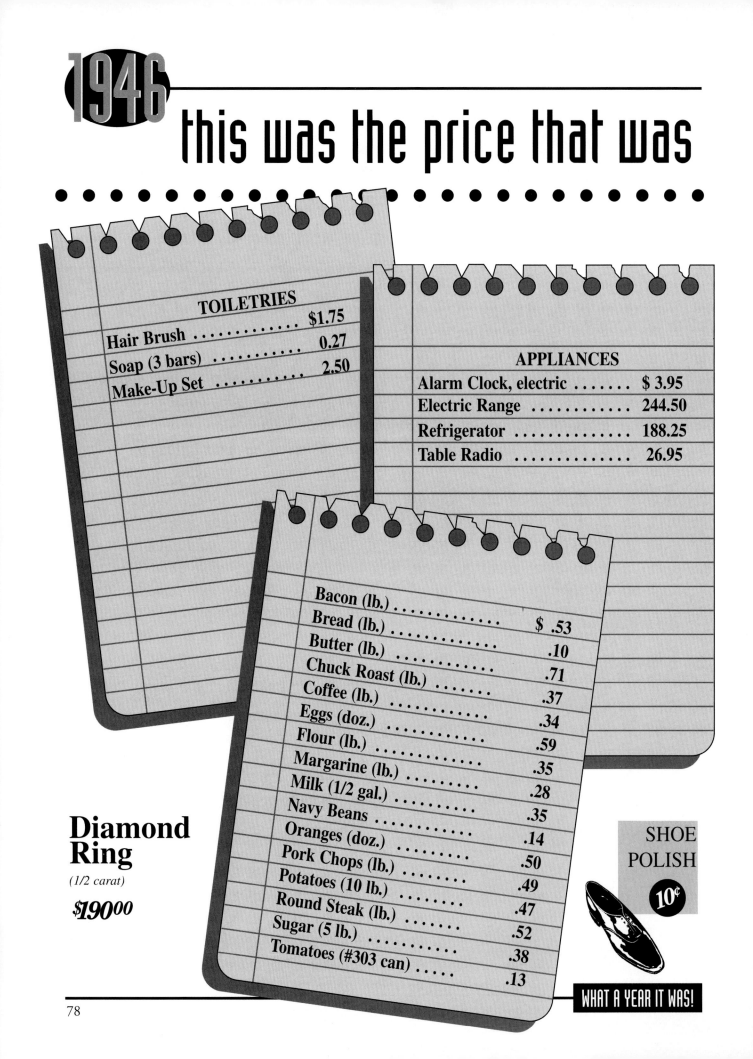

TOILETRIES

Hair Brush	$1.75
Soap (3 bars)	0.27
Make-Up Set	2.50

APPLIANCES

Alarm Clock, electric	$ 3.95
Electric Range	244.50
Refrigerator	188.25
Table Radio	26.95

Bacon (lb.)	$ .53
Bread (lb.)	.10
Butter (lb.)	.71
Chuck Roast (lb.)	.37
Coffee (lb.)	.34
Eggs (doz.)	.59
Flour (lb.)	.35
Margarine (lb.)	.28
Milk (1/2 gal.)	.35
Navy Beans	.14
Oranges (doz.)	.50
Pork Chops (lb.)	.49
Potatoes (10 lb.)	.47
Round Steak (lb.)	.52
Sugar (5 lb.)	.38
Tomatoes (#303 can)	.13

Diamond Ring

(1/2 carat)

$190⁰⁰

SHOE POLISH 10¢

WHAT A YEAR IT WAS!

Bridal Gown

$650.00

Women's •CLOTHING•

Bra	$ .79
Girdle	6.95
House Dress	1.95
Shoes	6.50

Men's Clothing

Hat	$ 12.50
Shirt	2.59
Shoes	10.50
Suit	27.00
Tie	3.50

SPORTS

Golf Bag and Clubs
$203.00

Tennis Racket
$22.00

Convertible Station Wagon
$2,890⁰⁰

This was a day in a dream

CHRISTMAS was today.

As long as I live I'll never forget this moment at the end of Christmas. The snow standing down there on our porch roof like a good meringue... the quiet twinkling stars (really twinkling).

And here, inside, this warm happiness stretching out under everything. Little Dickie tucked in bed between Old Mr. Teddy and New Mr. Teddy.

And Dick... just downstairs checking the lights and the fireplace... *not* on the high seas as he was *last* Christmas. What a thin gray day... with very sharp edges!

But today has been heaven... our house full of sunshine and talk and love and new toys

and more of our beautiful silver! Two new place settings in our own International Sterling pattern... now our set is complete!

How dear of Dick to think of it. I wrote him once that every time I set our table, the silver he and I had selected together was a sort of bridge... between the days when he was home and the time he'd be home again.

We have always been so proud of our International Sterling. So glad we selected the very best from the beginning. Dick couldn't have given me anything today that would have meant more — it's as though he had begun writing Part Two to our happiness.

Whenever you choose your "family" silver,

ask to see the International Sterling patterns.

Choose that one with your heart. As long as you live you'll enjoy its silver-solidness; the fine balance of each piece; the clear, beautiful design. Begin, if you like, with individual place settings: a knife and fork, teaspoon, salad fork, cream soup spoon, and butter spreader.

Prices on famous International Sterling have not been raised, even in the face of general rising prices. 6-piece place settings for as little as $21.50. All these patterns are made by The International Silver Company in the U. S. A.

TUNE IN to *The Adventures of Ozzie and Harriet*, Sunday Evening, 6:00 P. M., E.S.T., Columbia Broadcasting System.

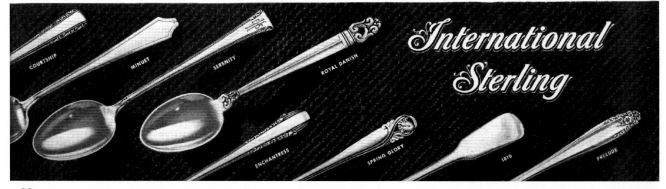

this was the price that was

AIRLINE FARES
FOR 1946

San Francisco to Boston	$125.10
New York to Los Angeles	118.30
Los Angeles to Chicago	85.45
Dallas to New York	66.15
Detroit to Oklahoma City	44.70
Washington, D.C to Chicago	27.25
Los Angeles to Phoenix	17.10
Toronto to Buffalo	3.20

Miscellaneous

Billfold, Ladies' . .	$4.50
Billfold, Men's	.5.00
Fountain Pen, Gold Tipped	.3.50

Household Items

Ironing Board	$ 6.95
Cedar Hope Chest	39.50
Blanket	6.45
Sheets	2.35
Sterling Silverware (6-piece place setting)	23.00

 PASSINGS

JOSEPH MEDILL PATTERSON,
Founder Of The New York Daily News, Dies at 67.

ARTHUR CHEVROLET,
One Of Three Swiss Brothers Who Made Automotive History, Dies at 61.

WHAT A YEAR IT WAS!

The last lovely touch to a lovely Boudoir . . .

Jewelite

PRACTICAL as they are beautiful, Jewelite combs, brushes and complete dresser sets will be cherished by every woman who cares for lovely things. Available in sparkling crystal or precious jewel colors, each article comes packaged in its own miniature showcase of transparent plastic. Ask for Jewelite at any good brush department. There are many kinds and grades of plastic, so be sure you get *genuine* Jewelite, the aristocrat of plastics. Pro-phy-lac-tic Brush Company, *Florence, Mass.*

Jewelite Roll-Wave Brush and Comb in delicate shades of ruby or sapphire, or diamond-clear crystal.

JEWELITE BY PRO-PHY-LAC-TIC

SCIENCE & MEDICINE

UNEXPLORED AREAS IN SCIENCE

✦ Living Longer, Healthier Lives

✦ Virus Conquests

✦ Psychological Disorders

✦ Exploration Of The Elements

✦ Exploration Of The Universe

✦ The Secret Of Photosynthesis

✦ The Secret Of Protoplasm

✦ Automatism

✦ Converting Psychological Warfare Into Psychological Welfare

■ The U.S. War Department Releases Report On Plans To Combat And Undertake Biological Warfare.

■ Rocket Engines Come Into Widespread Use In Experimental Aircraft And Guided Missiles.

NOBEL PRIZES

PHYSICS

Percy Williams Bridgman, For Work In High-Pressure Physics, U.S.

MEDICINE

Hermann J. Muller, For Study Of Mutations Under The Influence Of X-Ray Radiation, U.S.

CHEMISTRY

James B. Sumner, John H. Northrop, Wendell M. Stanley, For Work On Enzymes, All U.S.

1946

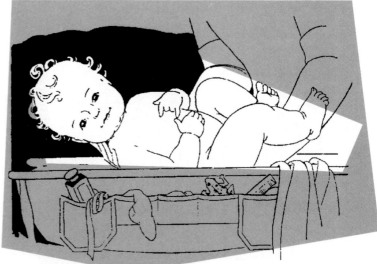

Medicine

◆ Dr. John Adriani, Head Of The Department Of Anesthesia At New Orleans' Charity Hospital, Develops New Procedure That Eliminates Painful Childbirth Through Injection Of Anesthesia Into Spinal Canal.

◆ Toads Replace Rabbits In Pregnancy Tests As They Give Results In Four Hours Instead Of Forty-Eight.

◆ Immunization Shots Against Whooping Cough And Diphtheria Recommended In The Last Trimester Of Pregnancy To Insure Immunity In The Newborn Against These Diseases During First Months Of Life.

◆ New Test Developed To Determine Pregnancy Through Monitoring Variation In The Body's Morning Temperature.

Rheumatic Fever
1 Number One Child Killer.

Medicine

Get Rid Of Those Saltshakers

✦ Salt Reduction Thought To Be Treatment For Stress Related Disorders.

✦ Recent Experiments Indicate That A Salt-Free Diet Will Help Some High Blood Pressure Patients.

Coffee, Maple And Vanilla Ice Cream Found To Be Excellent Sources Of Carotene And Riboflavin.

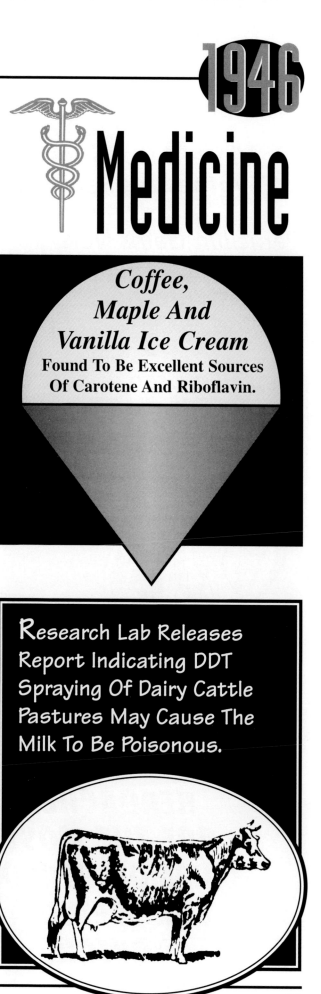

Research Lab Releases Report Indicating DDT Spraying Of Dairy Cattle Pastures May Cause The Milk To Be Poisonous.

Vitamin Deficiency Studies Conducted By Council On Foods And Nutrition Of The American Medical Association Reveal Symptoms of Such Deficiencies.

U.S. Chemist Vincent Du Vigneaud Synthesizes Penicillin.

•

Penicillin Gains New Stature As A Remedy Against Infectious Disease.

•

Penicillin Used Successfully In Curing Cattle Disease.

Food And Drug Administration Puts New Labeling Regulations Into Effect To Protect Consumers From Unsafe Non-Prescription Medicines.

HEADACHES ARE THE MOST COMMON REASON FOR SEEING A DOCTOR.

Hay Fever Sufferers Not Necessarily Neurotic

Dr. Earl R. Loew Discovers Benadryl, A Drug Which Brings Fast Relief For Hay Fever Sufferers And Victims Of Asthma And Hives.

Cancer Killed Twice As Many Americans As World War II.

Scientists Discuss Possible Link Between Smoking And Cancer At University Of Buffalo Symposium.

One Out Of Every Six Americans Is Infected With Trichinosis.

War Is Psychological Hell

- Psychological Study Released By The U.S. Army Indicates Psychiatric Casualties Are As Inevitable As Gunshot And Shrapnel Wounds And That Almost All The Men Who Fought In The North African Theatre Who Were Not Otherwise Disabled Ultimately Became Psychiatric Casualties.

- Paintings And Drawings By Battle Fatigued Veterans And People In Disturbed Psychological States Ignored In Clinical Research.

NURSES' DISCOVERY WINS GRATITUDE OF MILLIONS
— THE WORLD OVER !

What is the secret of the fabulous success of the "little blue jar" that you see everywhere— in millions of homes—in first-aid stations at beaches—in dressing rooms of Broadway stars —in barber shops—in army barracks all over the world? Here is the amazing story!

NURSES were among the first to discover the secret! Discovered that Noxzema is good for *so many* different things! Discovered that this soothing, snow-white, medicated cream brought quick relief to hands made rough and red by frequent washings—cooling comfort to burning, tired feet and to chafed, irritated skin—quick relief to unattractive, blemished complexions.

The news spread—until today, in millions of homes, Noxzema has become a "family first aid" for minor burns and scalds, for sunburn, for baby's diaper rash and chafing, for father's shaving irritations and many other externally-caused skin troubles. Thousands of girls use Noxzema as a night cream and powder base to help rough, dry skin become softer and smoother—free from ugly surface blemishes.

How does Noxzema do so much? It's a *medicated formula*—soothing, cooling, comforting—aids in faster healing. And it's greaseless—doesn't stain clothes.

Over 25,000,000 jars of Noxzema are used yearly in the U.S.—millions more in Canada and other countries. Perhaps *you* are one of its loyal friends. If not, *try* it. Sold at all drug counters.

GIRLS WITH "PROBLEM SKIN" find Noxzema *so* effective in helping heal ugly, externally-caused blemishes and for softening rough, dry skin. Thousands use it as a protective foundation.

RED, ROUGH, HOUSEWORK HANDS worry many a housewife. Thousands keep a jar of Noxzema in the kitchen to smooth and soften hands, help heal painful chapping and minor burns.

MOST POPULAR SUNBURN PREPARATION in America, Noxzema brings glorious, cooling, soothing relief to the red, tender skin; it's greaseless, non-sticky—doesn't stain clothes or bed linen.

DURING THE WAR, MILLIONS of men found Noxzema a real friend in need, bringing comfort to tired, burning feet, to skin burned by tropical suns, chapped by arctic winds, made raw and sore in wet, insect-infested jungles.

The fascinating 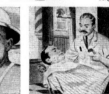 *story of Noxzema*

The Noxzema formula was developed by G. A. Bunting, D.Sc., of Baltimore; originally offered as a sunburn cream.

Nurses were the first to discover many new uses for Noxzema; today surveys indicate that 7 out of 10 nurses use Noxzema for themselves or patients.

For years, First-Aid Hospitals at Atlantic City, Coney Island, Miami, and other big beaches have made Noxzema a standard treatment for sunburn.

Barbers first used Noxzema as a base for lather for customers with tough beards— tender skin. Now there is a special Noxzema Shave Cream for hard-to-shave men.

Surveys show that 8 out of 10 Broadway show girls interviewed use Noxzema for soothing skin relief, to combat effects of make-up and to help keep complexion smooth, clear and attractive.

NOXZEMA  MEDICATED SKIN CREAM

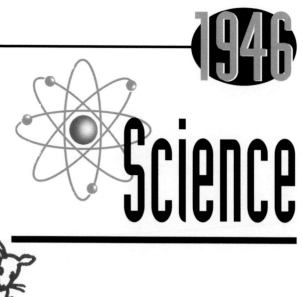

Science

The War Department Announces The Availability Of Radioactive Isotopes For Medical And Biological Research.

Glass Heart Tested On Laboratory Rats

DISCOVERIES

Underwater Islands Discovered Rising From Ocean Floor In The Pacific Between Hawaii and Marianas.

"Grand Canyon" Discovered In Mississippi Five Miles Wide With Walls More Than 600 Feet High.

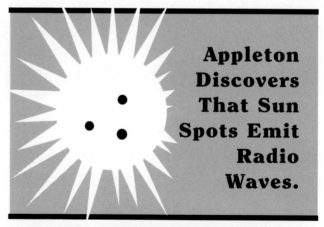

Appleton Discovers That Sun Spots Emit Radio Waves.

Research Reveals The Blood From Thoroughbred Horses Differs From Ordinary Horses.

SOVIET SCIENTISTS CLAIM THEY SPLIT THE ATOM.

Isotope Carbon 13 Discovered.

Hear that Click?
A NEW POINT-INSTANTLY!

C·L·I·C·K
C·L·I·C·K

Press the Magic Button with your thumb—
EVERSHARP REPEATER PENCIL
Feeds New Points Like a Machine Gun

AN EVERSHARP Repeater Pencil not only speeds your writing... it speeds your very thinking! There's no twisting or turning, no messy lead handling. It's a one-hand operation. Just press the Magic Button and it feeds new points automatically from a six months supply—that you drop in the barrel just as easily as dropping sugar into coffee!

New featherweight construction ends fin-ger strain—gives perfect balance for easier writing. EVERSHARP Repeater Pencils are priced from $1.50 to $50.
(Plus Federal Tax on pens $5 and over.)

Service Guaranteed Forever, If Your EVERSHARP Ever Needs Service, We Will Put It In Good Order For 35¢. This Service Is Guaranteed—Not For Years—Not For Life—But Guaranteed Forever!

TUNE IN Phil Baker in "TAKE IT OR LEAVE IT" — CBS, Sunday Night and *EVERSHARP's* Sensational New Show—Ann Sothern in "MAISIE" CBS, Wednesday Night.

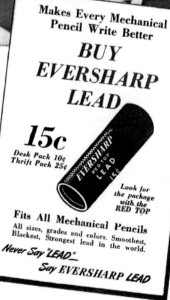

Makes Every Mechanical
Pencil Write Better
BUY
EVERSHARP
LEAD

15c
Desk Pack 10¢
Thrift Pack 25¢

*Look for
the package
with the
RED TOP*

Fits All Mechanical Pencils
All sizes, grades and colors. Smoothest, Blackest, Strongest lead in the world.

Never Say "LEAD"

Say EVERSHARP LEAD

Give **EVERSHARP**_*and you give the finest!*

© 1946, Eversharp, Inc.

90

INVENTIONS

Electronic Brain Built At Pennsylvania University.

Chester Carlson Invents Xerography.

Ford Motor Company Engineer Delmar S. Harder Devises System To Manufacture Engines And Coins The Word "Automation."

Grape Processing Machine Developed By Georges Monnet Of New York.

Westinghouse Electric Corporation Introduces Most Brilliant Electric Lamp Ever Developed For Commercial Use.

IBM Develops Fast Electronic Calculator "ENIAC" For The U.S. War Department. Model For Commercial Use Ready For Release.

Great Atlantic And Pacific Tea Company Solves Bread Mold Problem By Exposing Wrapped Bread To A High-Frequency Heat Generated In An Electric Oven.

The Dry Cleaning Industry Tries To Develop Technique For Cleaning Curtains And Draperies Made Of Fiber Glass

1946

inventions

Fairey Aviation Company Builds Pilotless Rocket Missile.

First Jet Fighter Plane Developed In Britain.

B-17 Bombers Fly From Hawaii To California Without A Crew, Controlled Entirely By Radio.

Pilot Ejector Seat Tested Successfully At Wright Field.

U.S. NAVY ANNOUNCES PLANS TO BUILD WORLD'S FIRST ATOMIC SUBMARINE

Self-Charging Portable Radio Designed To Operate For 20 Hours On A Penny's Worth Of Electricity Through The Use Of A 2-Volt Leak-Proof Rechargeable Battery Is Introduced.

General Electric Is Assigned Patent Rights To Refrigerator With Separate Ice-Cube Freezer Which Promises Greater Efficiency In The Development Of Tomorrow's Refrigerators Which Will Have Two Temperatures.

A Combination Automatic Radio And Electric Clock Replaces The Alarm Clock.

Rudolph F. Mallina Of Hastings-On-Hudson, New York Invents The Push-Button Telephone And Assigns Rights To The Bell Telephone Laboratories, Inc.

Mind If I Dunk?

The newest innovation for dunking a doughnut comes to us from Connecticut where a baker devised a doughnut with the usual hole in the middle but with a handle twisted like a cruller for an easy holding-and-dunking motion.

Anthony W. Delucchi Of Stockton, California Gets U.S. Patent On Design Of A Drive-In, Serve Yourself Restaurant.

General Electric And The Automatic Canteen Company Of America Develop An Electronic Vending Machine Which Dispenses Hot Food, Such As Hamburgers Or Hot Dogs For A Dime.

General Electric's "Traffic Master" Automatically Regulates Amount Of "Go" Time At Busy Intersections.

Hidden Automobile Burglar Alarm Developed By Fred E. Engler, Pukwana, So. Dakota.

Bell Telephone Announces Testing Of Mobile Radio-Telephone Service Along Three Interstate Highways.

Plane That Sheds Its Wings And Turns Into An Automobile Created By Aviation Engineer Ted Hall.

Start Easier!

Amazing New Oil...War-Proved in Army and Essential Equipment

NEW Mobiloil

Makes Engines Cleaner...Perform Better...Last Longer!

Keep Your Engine

Mobiloil Clean

1. "Mobiloil Clean" means that new improvements in Mobiloil keep rings, pistons, valves freer from deposits that waste power, fuel—vital working parts are cleaner.

2. New Mobiloil insures immediate oil distribution to all working parts—full delivery of liquid oil to heavily loaded bearings.

3. New Mobiloil permits quick starts —assures utmost protection against wear—provides efficiency and economy of operation evidenced by low oil and fuel consumption and minimum repairs.

New Mobiloil has been proved the hard way—in thousands of Army combat and transport vehicles—essential truck and bus fleets . . .

It's the finest Mobiloil ever made!

Don't just "change oil"—change to New Mobiloil at your Mobilgas dealer's.

SOCONY-VACUUM OIL CO., INC. and Affiliates: Magnolia Petroleum Co., General Petroleum Corporation of Calif.

TUNE IN "INFORMATION PLEASE"— MONDAY EVENINGS, 9:30 E.S.T.—NBC

inventions

New Electronic Device Measures Speed Of A Baseball.

American Machine and Foundry Co. Unveils Prototype Of Automatic Pinspotter, Beginning A Revolution In Bowling.

Transparent Mirror Allows An Observer To See His Reflection While Watching What's Happening On The Other Side Of The Pane.

New Device Which Translates Sound Into Visible Patterns Will Help The Deaf Learn To Speak.

Conveyor Belt Allows Rapid Unloading Of Cargo From Planes While In Flight.

Western Union Announces Plans To Replace Millions Of Miles Of Wire With Super High-Frequency Radio Beams.

GENERAL ELECTRIC CREATES LAMP THAT DUPLICATES ARTIFICIAL SUNLIGHT WITH TANNING AND WARMING CAPABILITIES.

New Lie Detector Invention Using Electrical Apparatus Developed By The Chicago Police Department.

Frank Lloyd Wright Unveils "Bizarre" Model For Manhattan's Guggenheim Gallery.

❖PASSINGS❖

John Baird Logie, Inventor Of "Televisor" (First Instrument To Transmit Scenes By Wire Or Wireless), Dies At 58.

Carlton C. Magee, Inventor Of The Parking Meter, Dies At 73

WHAT A YEAR IT WAS!

You don't stay <u>first</u> *unless* you're <u>best</u>

1915

"They won't work, and I'll prove it!" said a Detroit automotive engineer in 1913.

So he put a set of Goodyear's new multiple-cord tires on his car and set out for Indianapolis. To his amazement, he arrived there with the tires as good as new. Determined to prove his point, he wheeled onto the Speedway and tired himself out trying to wear out the tires.

His experience, and that of other drivers, proved that Goodyear had developed a tire which went 7500 miles instead of 2500! A tire which gave *3 times* the mileage of other tires! A tire so much better that by 1915 Goodyear became America's largest selling tire, and Goodyear went into first place in tire sales.

1946

"Ordered off okay," read the tags on this set of today's Goodyears.

And here's what that "okay" means: In one of the most brutal, rugged road tests ever given—in a test which wore out lesser tires one after another—these Goodyears clicked off 51,000 miles at an average speed of 60 miles an hour, and *were taken off still "okay!"*

Special test tires? No, sir! They're exactly the same tough Goodyears you'll find at your dealer's! No wonder Goodyear holds its place as America's first-choice tire for the 31st consecutive year!

Two versions of the world's finest tire:

De Luxe Rib Tread   De Luxe All-Weather* Tread

*T. M. The Goodyear T. & R. Co.

<u>First</u>-every year for 31 years

GOOD YEAR

*M*ore people ride on Goodyear tires than on any other kind

New Products

New Electronic Blanket Keeps Bed At A Constant Temperature All Night Long.

HOME INTER-COMMUNICATION SYSTEM GIVES MOM A NEW WAY TO KEEP AN EAR ON BABY.

Fully equipped, factory-fabricated houses selling for under $6,000 will be produced by Shelter Industries of New York.

2-Story Collapsible Trailer Offers An Answer To The Nation's Housing Problems.

New Lower-Priced Automatic Dishwashers Are Produced In A Factory That Formerly Made Cores For Armor-Piercing Bullets.

1946

MODERNISTIC NEW CARS

You said the engine is where??

These lovely ladies demonstrate the ease with which this car converts to a convertible.

The packages are placed in the trunk (yes, it's in the front), and off they go for a nice drive.

KAISER
SPECIAL
PRODUCT OF KAISER-FRAZER

TRAIL BLAZERS
IN
POSTWAR STYLING!
BUILT AT WILLOW RUN

ONLY ONCE in a decade comes a distinctly new trend in motor car styling—a trend so clearly in accord with public preference that it is only a matter of time until all manufacturers fall into line. The KAISER SPECIAL and the FRAZER, America's first 1947 motor cars, have set a trend in body styling, passenger comfort and driver convenience that will be reflected in other automobiles in the years to come. You can see *these* cars at your dealer's showroom now.

FRAZER
PRODUCT OF
GRAHAM-PAIGE

Window That Opens And Closes Like A Venetian Blind Designed By Hardin Manufacturing Company Of Los Angeles.

Claiming DDT Coated Wallpaper To Be Non-Hazardous To Human Beings And Domestic Animals, The Trimz Company Of Chicago Develops Line Of Wall Coverings Coated With DDT Guaranteed To Be Effective Against Insects For A Year.

New Products

Lightweight Fiber Glass Material Developed As Insulation For B-29's May Be Used As Lining In Jackets, Mittens And Sleeping Bags.

"Airtopia" System Developed By Drayer-Hanson Of Los Angeles Heats Or Cools, Cleans, Humidifies, Or Dehumidifies, And Circulates Air For Homes And Office Buildings.

Saks Fifth Avenue Buys Newly-Developed Estee Lauder Cosmetics.

Kaiser-Frazer Automobiles Are Introduced.

In all this new postwar world—

only the New Chevrolet brings you
Chevrolet's famous BIG-CAR QUALITY at lowest cost!

THE moment you see this beautiful new Chevrolet you'll know that Chevrolet has again kept faith with its millions of owners and prospective owners by giving them Big-Car quality at lowest cost in purchase price, operation and upkeep.

You'll recognize this Big-Car quality in the many vital features found only in Chevrolet and higher-priced cars, and also in *every* phase of Chevrolet design and construction.

Big-Car quality guides the selection of the basic materials. Big-Car quality governs all Chevrolet specifications. Big-Car quality

guards every manufacturing operation, every inspection, every test. And, of course, such quality means much to you—and to us.

To you, it means deep and abiding satisfaction with your motor car investment; and to us, it means a steady continuation of that long-term friendship and favor which you and millions of other buyers have given to Chevrolet.

Decide now to get Big-Car styling, Big-Car comfort, Big-Car quality, by purchasing a new Chevrolet—the *only* low-priced car with all the Big-Car quality features illustrated here.

CHEVROLET MOTOR DIVISION. *General Motors Corporation*, DETROIT 2, MICHIGAN

NEW CHEVROLET

102

YOU PUT IT FIRST IN SALES

CHEVROLET

WE KEEP IT FIRST IN VALUE

NEW BEAUTY-LEADER STYLING *with modern, streamlined, Door-Action fenders,* featuring new Wide-Wing radiator grille; new hood ornamentation; sparkling new color harmonies; and massive new "Car-Saver" bumpers, giving "round the fender" protection, both front and rear.

PROVED VALVE-IN-HEAD THRIFT-MASTER ENGINE

exclusive to Chevrolet in its price range, and giving an unequaled combination of performance and economy.

LUXURIOUS BODIES BY FISHER
with No Draft Ventilation

with smart, modern lines and contours, with roomy, richly upholstered interiors and with Concealed Safety Steps —by far the most beautiful and most comfortable bodies in the entire low-price field.

POSITIVE-ACTION HYDRAULIC BRAKES

for smooth, safe, positive stops.

EXTRA-EASY VACUUM-POWER SHIFT
with Syncro-Mesh Transmission

the simplest, quickest and easiest of all steering-column gearshifts.

UNITIZED KNEE-ACTION RIDE

giving riding smoothness and riding comfort exclusive to Chevrolet in the low-price field.

SHOCKPROOF STEERING

adding greatly to driving ease, driving comfort and driving safety.

NEVER HAS CHEVROLET BUILT A BETTER CAR THAN THIS **NEW CHEVROLET**

103

1946

New Products

Eastman Kodak Introduces Ektachrome — The First Color Film A Photographer Can Process Himself.

Vespa Motor Scooters Introduced In Italy.

Tide's In ... Dirt's Out

Procter & Gamble Introduces *Tide* To The Housewives Of America.

AT&T Announces Car-Phone Service In St. Louis.

❏ The New Westinghouse Laundromat Is A Front-Loading Machine Requiring Low-Sudsing Soap Or Detergent.

❏ Electric Clothes Dryer Hits The Consumer Market.

STILL TICKING AFTER ALL THESE YEARS...
Norwegian-American Entrepreneur Joakim Lehmkuhl, Wartime Producer Of Timing Mechanisms For Bomb And Artillery Shell Fuses, Introduces Timex Watches.

AND...

H. Hattori & Co. Present Seiko Watches.

WHAT A YEAR IT WAS!

ENTERTAINMENT

Oscar Night in Hollywood

Among the film notables attending this gala evening are:

Myrna Loy and Gene Markey *(top)*,

Margaret O'Brien *(center)* and

Ann Blyth and mom *(bottom)*.

Ingrid Bergman presents Ray Milland with the Best Actor Oscar for his role in "The Lost Weekend".

Ann Revere receives her Oscar for Best Supporting Player in "National Velvet".

Billy Wilder (left) and Charles Brackett win Oscars for Best Screenplay – "The Lost Weekend".

Jean Hersholt, representing the Board of Governors, presents Bob Hope with a mini-mini-mini version of the coveted Oscar as their way of saying "thank you" for acting as master of ceremonies for the last seven years.

MOVIES

BEST PICTURE

The Best Years Of Our Lives

BEST ACTOR

Fredric March,
The Best Years Of Our Lives

BEST ACTRESS

Olivia de Havilland,
To Each His Own

BEST DIRECTOR

William Wyler,
The Best Years Of Our Lives

BEST SUPPORTING ACTOR

Harold Russell,
The Best Years Of Our Lives

1946 Favorites (Oscars Presented In 1947)

BEST SUPPORTING ACTRESS

Anne Baxter,
The Razor's Edge

BEST SONG

"On The Atchison, Topeka And Santa Fe"

Columbia Pictures Announces Rita Hayworth's Wardrobe For "Gilda" Will Cost A Small Fortune — $60,000.

1946 births

Loni Anderson
Candice Bergen
Barry Bostwick
Cher
Connie Chung
Bill Clinton
Patty Duke
Sandy Duncan
Lola Falana
Werner Fassbinder
Sally Field

Joe Greene
Gregory Hines
Mary Beth Hurt
Reggie Jackson
Tommy Lee Jones
Naomi Judd
Diane Keaton
David Lynch
Barry Manilow
Liza Minnelli

Craig T. Nelson
Dolly Parton
Priscilla Presley
Linda Ronstadt
Susan St. James
Susan Sarandon
Talia Shire
Gene Siskel
Sylvester Stallone
Oliver Stone
Donald Trump
Twiggy
Ben Vereen
Lesley Ann Warren
Jann Wenner

RADIO

TOP 10 EVENING RADIO SHOWS

1. Jack Benny
2. Fibber McGee & Molly
3. Bob Hope
4. Charlie McCarthy Show
5. Fred Allen
6. Radio Theatre
7. Amos 'n' Andy
8. Walter Winchell
9. Red Skelton
10. Screen Guild Players

TOP 10 DAYTIME RADIO SHOWS

1. When A Gal Marries
2. Young Widder Brown
3. Our Gal Sunday
4. Portia Faces Life
5. Kate Smith Speaks
6. Ma Perkins
7. Breakfast In Hollywood
8. Aunt Jenny
9. Right To Happiness
10. Romance Of Helen Trent

WHAT A YEAR IT WAS!

Marie McDonald
"The Body"

Hollywood Types Its Beauties

Lizabeth Scott
Cafe-Society

Maureen O'Hara
Romantic

Lana Turner
Glamorous

Hedy Lamarr

Classical European

Despite Her Position As A Star, Ginger Rogers, Unlike Most Other Stars, Prefers To Do Her Own Movie Screaming Over Using A Professional Screamer.

- *Anna And The King Of Siam*
- *Beauty And The Beast* • *Blue Skies*
- *Brief Encounter* • *Cluny Brown*
- *Deception* • *Gilda* • *Great Expectations*
- *Green For Danger* • *It's A Wonderful Life*
- *My Darling Clementine* • *Notorious*
- *Odd Man Out* • *Open City*

WHAT A YEAR IT WAS!

MOVIES

- *Song Of The South*
- *Stairway To Heaven*
- *The Best Years Of Our Lives*
- *The Big Sleep*
- *The Harvey Girls*
- *The Jolson Story*
- *The Killers*
- *The Macomber Affair*
- *The Postman Always Rings Twice*
- *The Razor's Edge*
- *The Spiral Staircase*
- *The Yearling*
- *Three Little Girls In Blue*
- *Three Strangers*
- *Ziegfeld Follies*

WHAT A YEAR IT WAS!

France Holds First Cannes Film Festival.

"THE OUTLAW" Scheduled For Release After Three Years Of Tangling With The Censors Because Of Jane Russell's Abundant Bosom.

The Inimitable **W.C. Fields** Dies At 66 On Christmas.

PASSINGS

George "Slim" Summerville
Famed For His "Hick" Roles In Movies, One Of The Original Keystone Cops, Dies At 50.

William S. Hart
Western Movie Star, Dies At 73.

Noah Beery, Sr.
Stage & Screen Actor, Dies At 62.

WHAT A YEAR IT WAS!

MUSIC

1946

DECCA RECORDING STARS

Andrews Sisters

Carmen Cavallaro

Bing Crosby

Kenny Baker

Jimmy Dorsey

Charlie Barnet

Jimmy Durante

Connie Boswell

Kitty Carlisle

Deanna Durbin

Percy Faith

Ella Fitzgerald

Helen Forrest

Judy Garland

Glenn Gray

Lionel Hampton

Dick Haymes

Hildegarde

Jimmy Lunceford

Louis Jordan

Ink Spots

Guy Lombardo

Mary Martin

Mills Brothers

Burl Ives

Fred Waring

Russ Morgan

Victor Young

Ethel Smith

WHAT A YEAR IT WAS!

113

1946

The Famous Austrian Trapp Family Singers Give Annual Christmas Concert In New York's Town Hall.

Duke Ellington

Fans Turn Out In Record Number For Carnegie Hall Concert.

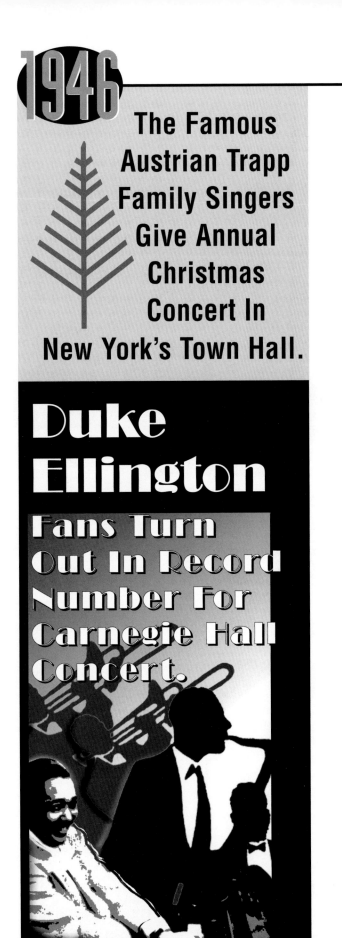

Woody Herman Fan Igor Stravinsky Writes 8-minute "Ebony Concerto" For Herman's Band.

PASSINGS

Vincent Youmans, Composer Of "Tea For Two", Dies At 47.

Harry von Tilzer, Who Coined The Name "Tin Pan Alley" And Wrote Such Hits As "I Want A Girl Just Like The Girl" And "Wait Till The Sun Shines, Nellie" Dies In Manhattan Of A Heart Attack At 73.

WHAT A YEAR IT WAS!

POPULAR SONG HITS

All Through The Day

Anything You Can Do

Aren't You Glad You're You

Come Rain Or Come Shine

Day By Day

Doctor, Lawyer, Indian Chief

Doin' What Comes Natur'lly

Five Minutes More

(Get Your Kicks On) Route 66

Golden Earrings

How Are Things In Glocca Morra

I Can't Begin To Tell You

I Don't Know Enough About You

I Got The Sun In The Morning

If This Isn't Love

I'm A Big Girl Now

It Might As Well Be Spring

It's A Good Day

La Vie En Rose

Linda

Let It Snow, Let It Snow, Let It Snow

Oh, What It Seemed To Be

Old Devil Moon

Ole Buttermilk Sky

Personality

Rumors Are Flying

Shangri-La

Shoo-Fly Pie And Apple Pan Dowdy

Some Day You'll Want Me To Want You

South America, Take It Away

Surrender

Tenderly

The Christmas Song

The Girl That I Marry

The Gypsy

The Old Lamp Lighter

There's No Business Like Show Business

They Say It's Wonderful

This Heart Of Mine

To Each His Own

When I'm Not Near The Girl I Love

You Always Hurt The One You Love

You Make Me Feel So Young

You're Nobody 'Til Somebody Loves You

Zip-A-Dee-Doo-Dah

Benjamin Britten's

"THE RAPE OF LUCRETIA"

Gian Carlo Menotti,

"The Medium"

BORIS BLACHER'S Chamber Opera

"Die Flut"

PULITZER PRIZE
LEO SOWERBY,
"The Canticle Of The Sun"

BENJAMIN BRITTEN'S OPERA, "PETER GRIMES," MAKES ITS AMERICAN DEBUT AT THE BERKSHIRE MUSIC FESTIVAL WITH LEONARD BERNSTEIN CONDUCTING.

Igor Stravinsky Premieres "Symphony In Three Movements" And Aaron Copland Introduces "Symphony No. 3".

WHAT A YEAR IT WAS!

"Madame Butterfly"

**Performed At The Met
For The First
Time Since
Pearl Harbor
With Record
Number Of
Fans Turned
Away At
Box Office.**

Samuel Barber's
"Concerto For Cello
And Orchestra"
Receives New York
Music Critics Circle
Award As The Best
New American Work
To Be Premiered In
New York.

Salzburg Festival Reopens

Pablo Casals Refuses Recital Invitations In America And England Because Of Their Recognition Of Franco's Spain.

Charles Ives

Veteran American Composer, Charles E. Ives, Receives Long Overdue Recognition As A Unique Phenomenon In Musical History.

George Szell Replaces Eric Leinsdorf As Cleveland Orchestra Conductor At A Salary Of $30,000 Yearly – Highest Ever Paid For That Job.

Arturo Toscanini, 78, Celebrates The 50th Anniversary Of The Premiere Of Puccini's "La Boheme" By Conducting The First Two Acts Over NBC Radio In What Is Hailed As The Best Performance Of The Opera In America Since He Conducted It At The Met In 1910.

Have Baton, Will Travel

1946

Three Young Conductors –
Leonard Bernstein, Bernard
Herrmann And Robert Lawrence
– Represent America Abroad.

Arturo Toscanini Conducts At
La Scala And Eric Leinsdorf
Tours Europe.

WHAT A YEAR IT WAS!

119

BALLETS

Frederick Ashton's "Symphonic Variations"

BALANCHINE'S "NIGHTSHADOW"

Under The Choreographic Direction Of George Balanchine, The Ballet Russe de Monte Carlo Winds Up Its Longest Run Of Ballet In Manhattan History.

THE BEST EVER

Harvard's Fogg Museum Mounts Most Comprehensive Pre-Raphaelite Show Ever Exhibited In The United States.

The Best Gauguin Show Ever Seen In The U.S. Mounted In A Manhattan Gallery.

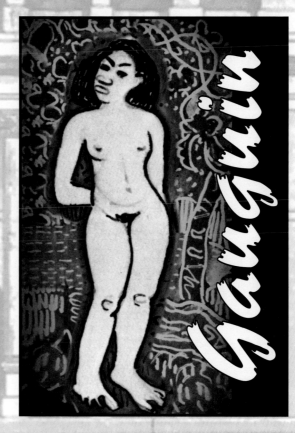

Young Sculptor, Charles Salerno, Debuts 14 Works To Critical Acclaim.

MAX BECKMANN

Max Beckmann's War Works Go On View In A Manhattan Gallery For The First Time.

GEORGIA O'KEEFFE
First Woman To Exhibit At The Museum Of Modern Art.

Hyman Bloom, Whose Works Appeared In The Museum Of Modern Art's Presentation, **AMERICANS-1942,** Holds His First One-Man Exhibition.

art

The U.S. War Department Stores 200 Masterpieces Valued At $80,000,000 Rescued From Destroyed Or Damaged German Museums Until They Are Returned To Germany Or The Rightful Owners.

Holland Sends America A "Garland Of Thanks" By Lending For Exhibition 48 Sixteenth And Seventeenth Century Dutch Masterpieces Stolen By The Nazis.

art

PAINTINGS

GRAHAM SUTHERLAND'S

"Thorn Trees,"
"Thorn Heads,"
"Thorn Head"
and "Crucifixion"

CHAGALL PAINTS "COW WITH UMBRELLA"

Fernand Leger Paints "Composition With Branch"

art

BILLY ROSE PAYS $75,000 FOR REMBRANDT'S "PILGRIM AT PRAYER" AT PARKE-BERNET AUCTION.

200 TOP U.S. ARTISTS REVEAL THEY EARN AN AVERAGE OF $1,154 A YEAR FROM THE SALE OF THEIR PAINTINGS.

PASSINGS

Photographer Alfred Stieglitz Dies At 82.

Joseph Stella, Hailed As An Artist Of Tomorrow, Dies At 69.

Art First Prize Winners In National Competitions *(A SAMPLING)*

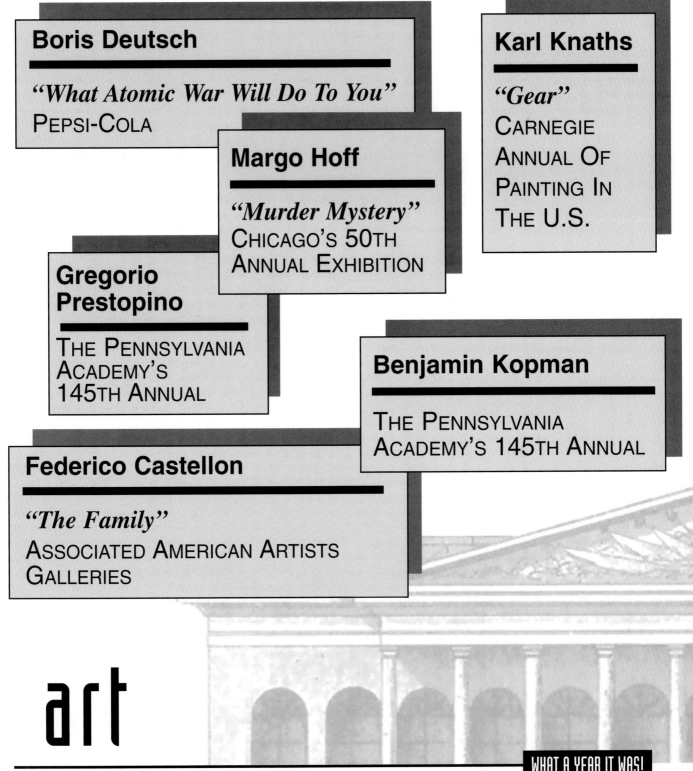

Boris Deutsch

"What Atomic War Will Do To You"
PEPSI-COLA

Karl Knaths

"Gear"
CARNEGIE ANNUAL OF PAINTING IN THE U.S.

Margo Hoff

"Murder Mystery"
CHICAGO'S 50TH ANNUAL EXHIBITION

Gregorio Prestopino

THE PENNSYLVANIA ACADEMY'S 145TH ANNUAL

Benjamin Kopman

THE PENNSYLVANIA ACADEMY'S 145TH ANNUAL

Federico Castellon

"The Family"
ASSOCIATED AMERICAN ARTISTS GALLERIES

art

OTHER WINNERS

Francis Barone Wins $1,500 Fellowship In Pepsi Cola's Third Annual Competition For His Painting Entitled: "Lime Kiln."

Ralston Crawford, Well-Known Abstractionist, Is Selected As The Only Artist-Correspondent To Witness The Bikini Tests.

art

In the "Wickedest City" in the World

this fiery-haired giant built an empire out of gunplay, gambling and the eager hearts of women!

This Sensational Best-Seller Has Already Thrilled More Than 650,000 Readers!

Yours for just a **3¢ Stamp**

when you join the Dollar Book Club

INTO the bawdy New Orleans of 1825—the "wickedest city in the world" —Stephen Fox plunged like a flaming sword, to wrest from the indolent Creole dandies and their soft, passionate women the money and power he had to have. Armed with nothing but a pearl he dared not sell and the trained hands of a gambler, he stole, cheated and slew until he had made himself a king, above the law and fearing not even God!

In Stephen Fox there was a steely will to conquer, and he rose from the muck of a pig boat to mastery of the greatest manor house in Louisiana by paying a high price—in other men's lives! He gambled and won like the card-sharp he was—until he found that to get the woman he wanted his skilled fingers must play to lose!

THE FOXES OF HARROW is as unusual a novel as you have ever read. It spotlights one of the most colorful regions in early America, during the tumultuous years between 1825 and the Civil War. It reveals a set of morals and customs that will make you ask in astonishment, "Was *that* America?" You will be fascinated by such vivid characters as Desiree, the lovely quadroon who gave Stephen Fox a red-haired son; Odalie, his wife who wanted her husband dead, and Little Inch, who was born a Negro slave and lived to become a master of men. No wonder THE FOXES OF HARROW has maintained a high place on the nation's best-seller list! Now, at the height of its popularity, this splendid new novel can be yours for only a 3c stamp when you join the Dollar Book Club!

THE FOXES of HARROW

"Here are love and lusts and greeds, quadroon balls, voodoo, pistols at dawn. Fresh and fascinating."— *St. Louis Globe Democrat.* "Explosion enough for three books. Highly flavored, exhilarating tale."— *Chicago Sun.*

FRANK YERBY

Dollar Book Club Membership Is FREE!

THE DOLLAR BOOK CLUB is the *only* book club that brings you newly printed, current books by outstanding authors for only $1.00 each. This represents a saving to you of 50 to 75 per cent from the established retail prices. Every Dollar Book Club selection is a handsome, full-sized library edition, well printed and bound in a format exclusively for members. You are privileged to purchase as many Club books as you wish at the special price of $1.00.

Although one outstanding book is chosen each month for exclusive distribution to members at $1.00 each, you do not have to accept a book every month; only the purchase of six a year is necessary. In fact, for convenience most members prefer to have shipped and pay for books every other month.

Outstanding new best-sellers by such popular authors as Mary Roberts Rinehart, Louis Bromfield, Somerset Maugham and Kenneth Roberts have been received by members at $1.00 each, while the public was paying from $2.50 to $3.00 for the publisher's edition at retail. A membership of more than 600,000 enables the Club to offer book values unequaled by any other method of buying.

Choose Your First Selection from These Best-Sellers

Upon receipt of the attached coupon with a 3c stamp you will be sent a copy of "The Foxes of Harrow." You will also receive as your first selection for $1.00 your choice of any of the following four best-sellers:

● *The King's General,* by Daphne du Maurier. The best-selling new historical romance by the author of *Frenchman's Creek* and *Rebecca.* A suspenseful tale of a charming rake and the slip of a girl he dared love.

● *The Strange Woman,* by Ben Ames Williams. The unforgettable story of a "Maine Cleopatra," by the author of *Leave Her to Heaven* — soon to be seen as a spectacular $2,000,000 movie starring Hedy Lamarr.

● *The Black Rose,* by Thomas Costain. The million-copy best-selling novel of the lovely harem girl whom Walter of Gurney risked death and torture to save — and for whose sake he pitted himself against the great Khan of the Orient!

● *Before the Sun Goes Down,* by Elizabeth Metzger Howard. He knew the whole town's secrets—yet hid a burning secret of his own! The $145,000 prize-winning novel of a small-town doctor and his strange, forbidden love.

Every other month you will receive the descriptive folder called The Bulletin, which is sent exclusively to members of the Club. The Bulletin describes the forthcoming two months' book selections and reviews ten or more additional titles (in the original publishers' editions selling at retail for $2.50 or more) available to members at only $1.00 each. If, after reading The Bulletin, you do not wish to purchase either or both of the two new selections for $1.00 each, you may notify the Club any time within two weeks so that the books will not be sent you. In any case, you may purchase any of the other titles offered for $1.00 each. There are no dues or membership fees at any time.

Send No Money—Mail Coupon with 3c Stamp

When you see "The Foxes of Harrow" and your first selection and consider that these books are typical of the values you will receive for only $1.00, you will realize the great advantages of free membership in this popular Club. Don't miss this wonderful offer. Mail the coupon now!

DOUBLEDAY ONE DOLLAR BOOK CLUB, GARDEN CITY, N. Y.

MAIL THIS COUPON

"The Foxes of Harrow" yours for 3c stamp!

DOUBLEDAY ONE DOLLAR BOOK CLUB
Dept. 9 L. M., Garden City, New York

Please enroll me free as a Dollar Book Club subscriber and send me at once "The Foxes of Harrow" for the enclosed 3c stamp. Also send me as my first selection for $1.00 the book I have checked below:

☐ The King's General ☐ The Strange Woman
☐ The Black Rose ☐ Before the Sun Goes Down

With these books will come my first issue of the free descriptive folder called The Bulletin telling about the two new forthcoming one-dollar book selections and several additional bargains which are offered for $1.00 each to members only. I am to have the privilege of notifying you in advance if I do not wish to purchase any of the following months' selections and whether or not I wish to purchase any of the other bargains at the Special Club price of $1.00 each. The purchase of books is entirely voluntary on my part. I do not have to accept a book every month—only six during the year to fulfill my membership requirement. I pay nothing except $1.00 for each selection received plus a few cents handling and shipping cost.

Mr.
Mrs.
Miss..
(PLEASE PRINT)

St. and No...

City and
Zone No..............................State.................

Occupation................................If under 21,
Age, please..............

*Same Price in Canada; 105 Bond St., Toronto 2, Canada

books

NOBEL PRIZE

LITERATURE

HERMANN HESSE
(Switzerland)

PULITZER PRIZE

HISTORY

ARTHUR M. SCHLESINGER, JR.
The Age Of Jackson

BIOGRAPHY

LINNY MARSH WOLFE
Son Of The Wilderness

PASSINGS

GERTRUDE STEIN,
Author And Patron Of The Arts,
Dies In France At 72.

H.G. WELLS,
Prolific Author Of Prophetic
Science Fiction Books Including
"The War Of The Worlds" And
"The Time Machine" Dies At 79.

BOOTH TARKINGTON,
Two-Time Pulitzer Prize
Winning Novelist And Playwright,
Dies At 76.

DAMON RUNYON
Dies At 62.

books

Leon Trotsky's "Stalin" Published In The U.S.

ALL THE KING'S MEN
Robert Penn Warren

ANIMAL FARM
George Orwell

ARC DE TRIOMPHE
E.M. Remarque

BABY AND CHILD CARE
Benjamin Spock

BACK
Henry Green

B.F.'S DAUGHTER
John P. Marquand

DEATH AND ENTRANCES
Dylan Thomas

DELTA WEDDING
Eudora Welty

HIROSHIMA
John Hersey

I THE JURY
Mickey Spillane

LADDERS TO FIRE
Anais Nin

MEMOIRS OF HECATE COUNTY
Edmund Wilson

MIRACLE DE LA ROSE
JEAN GENET

WHAT A YEAR IT WAS!

MR. BLANDINGS BUILDS HIS DREAM HOUSE
Eric Hodgins

RED ROSES FOR ME
Sean O'Casey

books

STALINGRAD
Theodore Plievier

THE ART OF PLAIN TALK
Rudolph Flesch

THE BERLIN STORIES
Christopher Isherwood

THE BIG CLOCK
Kenneth Fearing

THE CHRYSANTHEMUM AND THE SWORD
Ruth Benedict

THE FOXES OF HARROW
Frank Yerby

THE MEMBER OF THE WEDDING
Carson McCullers

THE PERENNIAL PHILOSOPHY
Aldous Huxley

THIS SIDE OF INNOCENCE
Taylor Caldwell

WILLOWAW
Gore Vidal

ZORBA THE GREEK
Nikos Kazantzakis

BROADWAY OPENINGS

theatre

Irving Berlin's
Musical Comedy
"Annie Get Your Gun"
Starring
Ethel Merman

ALL MY SONS
*Ed Begley (L) and
Arthur Kennedy*

CALL ME MISTER

*Betty
Garrett*

PLAYS

All My Sons

Annie Get Your Gun

Another Part Of The Forest

Born Yesterday

Brigadoon

Call Me Mister

Joan Of Lorraine

Lute Song

St. Louis Woman

The Devil's General

The Iceman Cometh

The Winslow Boy

1946

Pulitzer Prize

Russel Crouse & Howard Lindsay, "State Of The Union"

PASSINGS

Laurette Taylor, Stage Actress, Winner Of New York Drama Critics' Circle Award For Her Role As The Mother In "The Glass Menagerie," Dies At 62.

WHAT A YEAR IT WAS!

radio

- Proponents Of FM Radio Charge That AM Network And Independent Stations Are Trying To Hamstring The Progress Of FM Accessibility Which Many Agree Will Occupy A Major Place In The Future Of Radio.

- Cass Daley Becomes Radio's Most Popular Comedienne.

- CBS Announces One Of The First And Biggest Buyers Of Soap-Opera Time, Procter & Gamble, Renewed Four Long-Running Programs – *Ma Perkins*, *Road Of Life*, *Life Can Be Beautiful* And *Young Dr. Malone* For Another Season.

- Zenith Radio And Its President, Commander Eugene F. McDonald, Jr., Support WWZR-FM In Chicago To The Tune Of $75,000 Yearly To Offer Radio Listeners A Commercial-Free, Music-Only Alternative To The Roar Of Commercial Radio.

- Abe Burrows, Called The Greatest Living Satirist By The Late Robert Benchley, Begins Writing A New CBS Comedy Show Called *Holiday & Co.* For A Salary Of $3,000 Weekly.

- Massive Panic, Including Suicides, Results From French National Radio Broadcast Of Tongue-In-Cheek Bulletins Announcing Accidental Atomic Explosions Were Shattering Cities And Destroying The World.

- Removal Of Wartime Restrictions Unleashes An Unprecedented Demand For New Or Augmented Radio Services.

- Bing Crosby Signs Contract For New International Radio Program At $30,000 Weekly – The Highest Salary Ever Paid For A Program Of This Type.

- Frank Stanton Elected President Of CBS.

65,000 Hats

Are Entered In Hedda Hopper's Hat Contest.

Dr. Peter C. Goldmark, 39-Year Old Inventor Of Color Television, Introduces Post-War Equipment That Produces Vivid Colors Prompting CBS To Announce The Seemingly Unsolvable Problems Had Been Solved And That If The Demand Is There, Color Television Could Be Enjoyed In American Homes Within A Year.

CBS
Builds New Television Receiver Compatible With Black And White And Color Transmissions.

AMERICAN FEDERATION OF MUSICIANS BARS ITS MEMBERS FROM TELEVISION PERFORMANCES PENDING INVESTIGATION INTO THE IMPACT ON THE RADIO INDUSTRY.

Construction Of Television Transmitter Completed On Mt. Wilson, California Extends Reception Radius To 100 Miles – Three Times The Radius Of A Lowland Station.

PASSINGS

Edward E. "Major" Bowes, "Patron Saint" Of Amateurs In The Entertainment World, Dies At 71.

WHAT A YEAR IT WAS!

DISASTERS

CHICAGO: Fire At LaSalle Hotel Causes 61 Deaths.

NEW YORK CITY: Fire Destroys Staten Island Ferry Terminal, Causing $2 Million Damage And Claiming 2 Lives.

NEW YORK CITY: 5 Killed When Army Plane Lost In Fog Crashes Into 58th Floor Of Building On Wall Street.

1946

MOUNT TAKI,
the famed Japanese
crater on the southern-
most tip of Kyushu
Island erupts after being
dormant for 32 years.

Moving down the slope at the rate of 10 yards per
hour, the molten lava threatens everything in its path.

The violent explosions endanger the city of Kagoshima, five miles across the Bay of Tanegashima.

Villages on the crater side of the bay are evacuated and the inhabitants watch the fireworks from a safe distance.

HUNDREDS DIE AS TIDAL WAVE RIPS HAWAII

Worst Disaster Since Pearl Harbor

A series of giant waves, varying from 30 to 50 feet high, originating in submarine earthquakes off the Alaskan coast travelled 2,500 miles to Hawaii at an incredible speed of 300 miles per hour and struck in the early morning hours.

The city of Hilo is hardest hit by a wave that smashes into the north side of the island, virtually demolishing the town of 25,000.

With 90 people dead and many more unaccounted for, the army helps in rescue operations.

1946

TURKEY: 1,330 Killed, Villages Leveled By Earthquake.

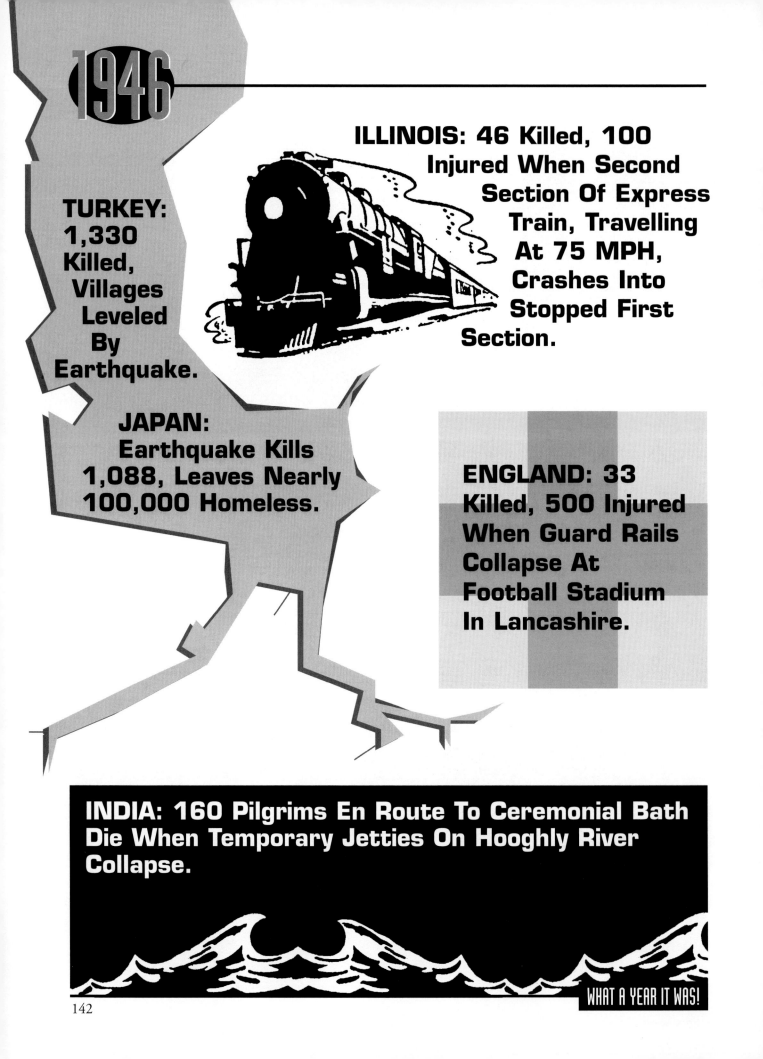

ILLINOIS: 46 Killed, 100 Injured When Second Section Of Express Train, Travelling At 75 MPH, Crashes Into Stopped First Section.

JAPAN: Earthquake Kills 1,088, Leaves Nearly 100,000 Homeless.

ENGLAND: 33 Killed, 500 Injured When Guard Rails Collapse At Football Stadium In Lancashire.

INDIA: 160 Pilgrims En Route To Ceremonial Bath Die When Temporary Jetties On Hooghly River Collapse.

WHAT A YEAR IT WAS!

FASHION

The fashion industry meets the challenge of lavish social activities and using materials scarce during the war such as silk, satin, linen and lace produces some of the most elegant, luxurious clothing seen since the Roaring 20's. American designers scale the heights in ingenuity and receive international recognition for their creations.

1946

The American Female – The Look

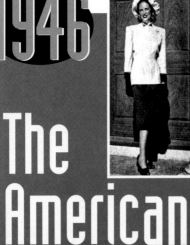

This suit combines a beige jacket with dark brown skirt.

A copper-colored wool using diagonal closing.

The look ranges from hip-length jackets, squared at the shoulders to shorter jackets with sash ties to rounded at the shoulders narrowing at the waist and hips.

Long Skirts Legalized With The Repeal Of Austerity Measure L85.

With Their Men Now Back From The War, Women Spend A Record $1.5 Billion For Their Easter Outfits.

Straw hats return for the first time since the war began and are trimmed with flower, feather and jewel decorations.

With the introduction of the strapless bra, the new bare-shouldered look becomes the fashion for evening.

WHAT A YEAR IT WAS!

A "MALLORY MATCH" Makes Time!

Inside this coat of smart sports plaid
You'll be a happy gent, m'lad.

Just park this lightweight felt aloft
And make the stoniest heart turn soft

Brunettes or blondes, they're all the same,
When a "Mallory Match" applies the flame!

The Dallas $15.00
IN PLIAFELT

● The way she looks *at you* depends on how you look *to her!*

So start that important week end right, with a good-looking suit and carefully matched accessories. And be sure to top off your outfit with a handsome DALLAS by Mallory.

You'll discover this all-American lightweight with a Texas accent has everything it takes. It's made in *Pliafelt*, too—Mallory's exclusive process that makes a hat superbly soft and crush-resistant.

Visit your Mallory dealer soon to select *your* DALLAS.

At fine men's stores everywhere

MALLORY
hats

STYLE LEADERS FOR 129 YEARS

145

1946 ADVERTISEMENT

Two ways to show up to advantage

1. The two men above are headed in different directions, but they'll both show up looking their best.

To do as well by yourself, you needn't have a house full of clothes, or even spend a lot of money. Just pick your clothes sensibly, with an eye to where you'll wear them.

Then, when you're headed for a big time, as these two are, you'll be set with an outfit that's right for the occasion —even to a smart new Stetson Narrow Brim hat...

2. The lad on the left is out to meet his date in a single-breasted, blue-gray sharkskin suit. His crisp blue-and-white striped shirt sets off his blue polka-dot tie to a T. And the crowning touch is one of the new Stetson Narrow Brim hats, blending quiet, good taste with a youthful air. This Stetson is the Vogue, in popular Caribou Gray.

3. The gent with the girl is headed for a party carrying a light brown diagonal-weave topcoat, and wearing a double-breasted dark brown suit with a narrow pin stripe. His shirt is white—his tie, a lively small print of red, black and yellow. The hat is the distinguished Stetson Diplomat, with narrow brim, in handsome Arabian Brown.

STETSON Narrow Brim Hats — Right for dressing up

The name Stetson in a hat is your assurance of quality and style. Stetson hats are made only by John B. Stetson Company and its subsidiary companies—in the United States and Canada.

146

The American Male— The Look

Men's fashion is predominantly still conservative in its look consisting of dark gabardine suits and sack coats without vests. More elaborate patterns and brighter colors are used in the newer worsted suits. Hats are narrow brimmed with high crowns.

Apparel Arts Names Best Dressed Sailor
Fleet Admiral Ernest J. King

1946

Newest headbands for bangs: black lace on black velvet ribbon, decorated with bows.

With Nylon Material Being Less Scarce, The Nylon Dress Which Does Not Require Ironing After Washing, Becomes Popular.

French Couturier Louis Reard Introduces Two-Piece Bikini Which Is Banned At Biarritz And Other Resorts.

1946 ADVERTISEMENT

FURS BY GUNTHER

" No wonder smart women are so pleased "

"Naturally every woman wants to look her best . . . whether the weather man says deep snow or light rain. So I'm delighted that high fashion Hood Raintogs are back! Those wonderful Talon Boots . . . those heavenly sleek Galoshes! My how light and flexible and stretchable they are—they fit perfectly over your shoes, yet they're so easy to get on and off. And for showery weather, what could be smarter than the light, comfortable, unlined Hood Oxfords? And they come in various heel heights to fit any of your shoes. See them at your dealer's."

1946 ADVERTISEMENT

Are you in the know?

When you don't know the routine, would you—

☐ Try it anyway
☐ Say your feet hurt
☐ 'Fess up frankly

Why lumber through a rumba—or spoil a jitt-bug's "shine?" If you aren't hep to the step, say so. 'Fess up frankly. Droons rush in where smoothies fear to tread. But at "certain" times, there's one fear a smooth girl can forget (with Kotex): the fear of telltale outlines. That's because Kotex has *flat tapered ends* that *prevent* revealing outlines. And you can dance the hours away in *comfort*, for Kotex is made to *stay soft while wearing.* (See how much longer that softness lasts!)

For camouflaging freckles, do you—

☐ Take the cake
☐ Apply lemon juice
☐ Wear a dotted veil

Freckle-heckled? To camouflage the summer's sun spots—take the cake (*makeup,* that is) and apply with wet sponge. Blot surplus with a Kleenex tissue; blend well with fingertips while damp. Then let dry —and you've got 'em covered! It's easy, when you know how. Like keeping dainty on problem days. You'll know how to stay dainty, charming, when you let Kotex help. Each Kotex napkin contains a *deodorant*— locked inside so it can't shake out!

How would you give your order?

☐ To the waiter
☐ To your escort
☐ Let your date choose your dinner

If you're a menu mumbler—speak up, sis! Choose what appeals to you (without blitzing his allowance), then tell it to your escort; he'll pass it on to the waiter. Be sure of how to order and be safe from embarrassment. That's one for your memory book. It's something to remember, too, when choosing sanitary protection. Choose Kotex, because Kotex has an exclusive *safety center* that gives you *plus* protection, keeps you *extra* safe—and confident!

More women choose KOTEX* than all other sanitary napkins

A DEODORANT in every Kotex* napkin at no extra cost

1946

TEENAGER LOOKS

CASUAL:
Blue Jeans
Flannel Shirt
Moccasins
(Replacing Saddle Shoes)

Wool jacket over blouse and skirt.

Printed crepe scarf blouse tied at waistline.

Basic blouse and full skirt cinched at waist with fabric belt and matching bolero jacket.

149

1946 ADVERTISEMENT

Clothes by Monte-Sano

Wedding-Cake Crowns

Tiered high, higher, highest for a wonderful new look.
Sharpening the excitement of the year's softer suits. Marking you
in the vanguard of a fresh fashion trend. Doubly good in
the new Stetson ceramic colors.

HORIZON GOLD . . . *cuff-brimmed, double-crowned for twice the smartness.* $16.95 *(Dark colors,* $14.95)
LACQUER GREEN . . . *a new swirled toque, sleek above your furs.* $15.95 *(Light colors,* $17.95)
CALIFORNIA BURGUNDY . . . *triple tiers of fine Stetson felt.* $16.95 *(Light colors,* $18.95)

STETSON HATS

1946

Miami Models Sport Newest Bonnet Fashions All Constructed From Materials Purchased From The Local Hardware Store.

A snappy little mouse-trap model.

Strainers trimmed with fish scalers.

Tin plate, strainers and oil can.

A bird with ping pong balls nestled in a steel wool nest.

This miniature cannon ends the show with a big bang.

This tweed suit with classic lines is set off by a finger-length coat.

Suits once again are designed with small collars and many are belted at the waist and are finished off with embroidery trim.

WHAT A YEAR IT WAS!

Double breasted coat made of soft wool in a light sepia color with round shoulders and full sleeves tight at the wrist.

Grey-beige gabardine finger-tip coat with detachable hood.

With restrictions lifted on many fabrics, the billowing sleeve becomes a fashion statement.

Dress necklines are either very high or provocatively low and small waistlines are emphasized.

The basic black dress is revitalized with the addition of peplums.

I'm Easier to Know—When You Use
MENNEN SKIN BRACER

Its He-Man Aroma WOWS the Ladies!

FOR ANY CLOSE-UP
THESE 10 SECONDS
MAKE THE DIFFERENCE THAT COUNTS

CALL it magic if you will. But you can chalk up that look in her eyes to the he-man aroma of Mennen Skin Bracer. It "wows" the ladies!

Try Mennen Skin Bracer after your next shave. Splash it on your chin, neck, and face. Enjoy its "wake-up" tingle. Helps heal tiny razor nicks. See how it tones up your skin . . . gives you a more youthful, more vigorous appearance. No wonder more men use Mennen Skin Bracer than any other after-shave lotion in America.

So, for those all-important close-ups, get Mennen Skin Bracer. Enjoy it after your next shave. See if she doesn't say "you're nice to be next to."

KEEP PRESENTABLE LONGER
Use Mennen Brushless Shave Cream for faster, cooler, more comfortable shaves! Actual surveys prove it's *first choice* with dermatologists (doctors specializing in the care of the skin). Creamier, easier to use.

SPECIAL FOR LATHER SHAVERS
Choose Mennen Plain or extra-cool Menthol-Iced! Fast-acting lather wilts whiskers . . . helps your razor glide along on *wings!* See how well groomed your face *looks* and *feels.*

SPORTS

1946

A Million And A Half People Line Up To Watch The 57th Annual Tournament Of Roses Parade In Pasadena.

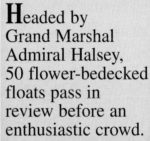

Headed by Grand Marshal Admiral Halsey, 50 flower-bedecked floats pass in review before an enthusiastic crowd.

San Francisco, United Nations Charter City, wins the prize for best depicting the theme of the pageant: Victory, Unity and Peace.

ROSE

Later in the day, 93,000 fans jam the Rose Bowl to watch the classic struggle between Southern California and Alabama.

With Admiral Halsey looking on, Harry Gilmer picks up 12 yards for the Crimson Tide.

BOWL

34-14!

With Gilmer's long pass, the Crimson Tide whomps Southern California 34-14.

Football

■ **Two Million Ticket Requests Turned Down For Army-Navy Football Game.**

■ **National Football League Games Set New Record For Attendance With 2,671,696 Fans Turning Out.**

■ **First Major Scandal Hits Professional Football With The Discovery Of An Attempt To Bribe Two Leading Players Of The New York Football Giants To Throw The Playoff Championship Game With The**

NEW RULES IN FOOTBALL

■ Number Of Time Outs Allotted To Each Team In Each Half Increases From Three To Four.

■ Larger Numbers On Uniforms Are Mandated.

Chicago Bears Beat Giants 24-14 For NFL Title.

ARMY BEATS NAVY 21-18 IN PHILADELPHIA.

HEISMAN TROPHY WINNER:
Glenn Davis (Army)

■

COACH OF THE YEAR:
Earl "Red" Blaik (Army)

Baseball

Connie Mack Heads Spring Training For The Athletics In West Palm Beach

The pitching team lines up for practice.

1946

Spring Training

Dick Fowler (top, right), Bobo Newsom (top, left) and Russ Christopher (right) go through their paces.

Baseball's grand old man, Connie Mack, can still show the guys a thing or two.

WHAT A YEAR IT WAS!

JUNE

8 Members Of Spokane's International League Baseball Team Are Killed As Their Chartered Bus Plunges Down A 500-Foot Mountainside In The Cascades.

JULY

14 Chicago White Sox Are Kicked Out Of Game For Heckling Umpire.

AUGUST

All 8 American And National League Baseball Games Played At Night For The First Time In History.

NEW YORK YANKEES

Sign Contract With United Air Lines Making Them First Baseball Team To Travel By Air For The Entire Season.

BASEBALL

 In the eighth inning of the first game of a doubleheader between the New York Giants and the Pittsburgh Pirates, Giants' manager, Mel Ott was ejected by umpire Tom Dunn.

During the fifth inning of the second game, Ott protested a decision by umpire George Magerkurth and was again thumbed from the game, thus becoming the first major league manager to be thrown out of both ends of a doubleheader.

83-Year Old Connie Mack Separates From His Second Wife, Katherine.

WHAT A YEAR IT WAS!

St. Louis Defeats Boston 4-3 And Takes The World Series.

MOST VALUABLE PLAYER

AMERICAN LEAGUE
Ted Williams (Boston)

NATIONAL LEAGUE
Stan Musial (St. Louis)

American League Wins Baseball's All-Star Game.

Shortstop JOSEPH TINKER *And 2nd Baseman* JOHN J. EVERS *Admitted To Baseball's Hall Of Fame In Cooperstown, N.Y. Along With 1st Baseman* FRANK CHANCE, *Who Died 22 Years Ago.*

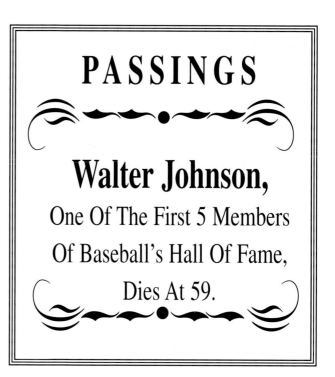

PASSINGS

Walter Johnson,
One Of The First 5 Members
Of Baseball's Hall Of Fame,
Dies At 59.

1946

POCKET BILLIARDS

Jimmy Karras *(above right)* and World's Pocket Billiards Champ Willie Mosconi demonstrate special cue artistry as their cross-country match ends in Chicago.

Irving Crane Of Livonia, New York Regains World Pocket Billiards Championship.

WHAT A YEAR IT WAS!

While an appreciative audience looks on, Karras demonstrates Chinese billiards and some tricky moves.

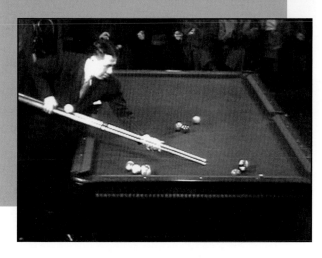

1946

U.S. TABLE TENNIS CHAMPIONSHIPS HELD AT ST. NICHOLAS ARENA, NEW YORK CITY

This participant demonstrates some pretty fancy footwork.

Men and women of all ages gather to compete for national table tennis honors.

TENNIS

DAVIS CUP Tennis Competition Resumes In Melbourne After 6 Years' Interruption Because Of The War, With The United States Team Defeating Australia 5-0.

U.S. LAWN TENNIS

Men's Singles
JOHN A. KRAMER
Women's Singles
PAULINE M. BETZ

WIMBLEDON

Yvon Petra Beats Geoff Brown

DAVIS CUP

U.S. Team Of Jack Kramer And Ted Schroeder Wins Davis Cup, Beating Australian Team.

Pauline Betz Wins Over Althea Brough.

GOLF

GOLFER BEN HOGAN DISCHARGED FROM THE ARMY.

BYRON NELSON LOSES UNITED STATES OPEN GOLF TITLE WHEN HIS CADDIE ACCIDENTALLY KICKS HIS BALL.

CHAMPIONS

U.S. OPEN: *Lloyd Mangrum*
PROFESSIONAL GOLFER'S ASSOCIATION: *Ben Hogan*
MASTERS TOURNAMENT: *Herman Keiser*
U.S. GOLF ASSOCIATION: *Ted Bishop*
BRITISH OPEN: *Sam Snead*

WHAT A YEAR IT WAS!

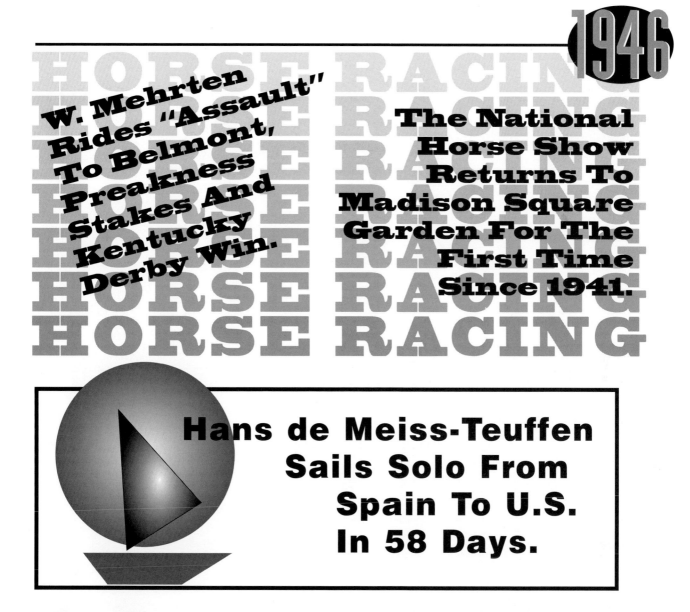

HORSE RACING
HORSE RACING
HORSE RACING
HORSE RACING
HORSE RACING
HORSE RACING
HORSE RACING

W. Mehrten Rides "Assault" To Belmont, Preakness Stakes And Kentucky Derby Win.

The National Horse Show Returns To Madison Square Garden For The First Time Since 1941.

Hans de Meiss-Teuffen Sails Solo From Spain To U.S. In 58 Days.

U.S.S.R.'s Mikhail Botvinnik Takes Over Position As World's Best Chess Player On The Death Of Aleksandr Alekhine.

John B. Kelly, Jr. (Brother Of Grace Kelly) Succeeds His Father As National Champion, Single Sculls.

WHAT A YEAR IT WAS!

BOXING

20,000 fans jam New York's Madison Square Garden for the Golden Gloves Tournament of Champions.

Ezra Gooderham, from West Virginia, (right) fights Tony Borselino from Newark, New Jersey.

WHAT A YEAR IT WAS!

■ **Tickets For Heavyweight Boxing Championship Bout Between Joe Louis And Billy Conn Soar To A Record High Of $100 Each.**

■ **Joe Louis Successfully Defends His World Heavyweight Boxing Title For the 22nd Time.**

■ **Couture Knocks Out Walton With One Punch In 10.5 Seconds Making It The Shortest Recorded Boxing Match In History.**

Gooderham K.O.'s Borselino with a mean wallop.

PASSINGS

Jack Johnson,
Former Heavyweight Champ,
Dies At 68.

1946

SPORTS EVENTS RETURN

Fans gather to watch the first races to be held in seven years, happy to return to peaceful pursuits.

A post-war steering device is only one of the novelties in this tandem race.

WHAT A YEAR IT WAS!

TO VIENNA

The motorcycle race has the usual chills, thrills and spills.

AUTO RACING

George Robson Wins Indy 500 At 114.8 MPH.

BOWLING

Andy Varipapa Wins The All-Star Match-Game Championship In Chicago. In A 90-Day Marathon Of Bowling, Contestants Have To Throw 64 Games Across The Alleys.

HOCKEY

Montreal Beats Boston To Take The Stanley Cup.

1946 WAS A GREAT YEAR, BUT...

THE BEST IS YET TO COME!

PHOTOGRAPHY CREDITS

All photographs are courtesy of **FlikBaks**™ unless they are listed below. The author gratefully acknowledges the following contributions: